The First Book of
C

The First Book of

C

Charles Ackerman

A Division of Macmillan Computer Publishing

11711 North College, Carmel, Indiana 46032 USA

*To Carol, who knows nothing about C and will probably keep
it that way even with this book.*

International Standard Book Number: 0-672-27354-3
Library of Congress Catalog Card Number: 90-63939

Acquisitions Editor: *Gregory Croy*
Production Editor: *Kathy Grider-Carlyle*
Indexer: *Hilary Adams*
Cover Artist: *Held & Diedrich Design*
Technical Reviewer: *Greg Guntle*
Production Assistance: *Martin Coleman, Sandra Grieshop, Tami Hughes, Bill Hurley, Betty Kish, Bob LaRoche, Sarah Leatherman, Kim Leslie, Howard Peirce, Cindy Phipps, Joe Ramon, Tad Ringo, Dennis Sheehan, Louise Shinault, Bruce Steed, Johnna VanHoose, Lisa Wilson, Christine Young*

Printed in the United States of America

Contents

vi

vii

viii

ix

Introduction

This member of the *First Book of* series by SAMS is designed around a proven format that introduces a complex subject to a beginning user in simple, easy steps. You should be able to understand the book better if you understand how the book was designed and written.

How The Book Is Organized

This book is written for someone who has never programmed in C before. We also presume the reader has never programmed in any language. You can learn the basics of computer programming in the first chapter. If you already program in another language, say BASIC or even dBASE, you can skim the first chapter and plunge into the second, which is where you write your first C program.

Each section of the book is designed around a discrete operation. For example, this *Introduction* introduces the book. The next chapter provides an overview of programming in general, describes where the C programming language fits into the scheme of all computer languages, and provides an introduction to the more popular C programming language programs for microcomputers. Each chapter after that teaches you a specific aspect of the C programming language using examples. They demonstrate how aspects covered in the chapter work by providing examples of C code you can copy, compile, and run for your own experience. You can then modify the code for your own use.

The end of this book contains appendixes that describe general information about the C programming language, such as keywords, functions, and library functions. You don't need this information to start learning how to program in C, but the information can be helpful for reference, or when you want to expand your knowledge about programming in C.

How The Book Was Written

The style of this book is geared toward the beginning programmer. Readers who are new to programming, or new to programming with the C language, will find this book most appropriate. *The First Book of C* teaches you how to program in C by example. There's no better way to learn a new subject than to work your way through it using simple step-by-step examples.

There are three levels for each chapter. First, you'll learn a specific concept, such as hex and decimal sets. Next, you'll be given an example of program code that demonstrates the concept. You write this code in the C editor of your choice, then compile it, and see how it runs. When the program works for you, we will walk you through the code line-by-line, so that you understand how it works.

There are several features appearing in this book that you should know about.

▶ You'll occasionally run across the names of keys, such as Enter. The Enter key is the big key on the right side of your keyboard usually marked "Enter" with a downward and left-pointing arrow. Because the instructions in this book pertain primarily to typing in character commands, you won't find too many references to specific keys. Each proprietary C program, such as Turbo C++ and QuickC, employs your keyboard keys in its own specific way.

▶ Options are listed and preceded by a bullet, just like this list of format features.

▶ The characters you type are case specific. That is, you should adhere to the uppercase and lowercase spelling used for various C commands, keywords, and other items. While case doesn't make a difference when you type commands at your DOS prompt, case does make a difference when you work in the C programming language.

What You Need To Use This Book

You can learn about programming in C, *theoretically*, by reading this book and doing nothing else. Ideally, however, this book has been designed to let you learn how to program in C using hands-on examples.

This means you should have any member of the IBM PC family, including the IBM PC XT or IBM PC AT, a PS/2, or any of the personal computers that are compatible with these brand-name IBM computers. On your computer you should have installed a standard C language compiler including a linker, the ANSI standard header files (see Appendix C), and an editor that lets you create clean ASCII text files.

For the examples in this book, we use the Windows 3.0 Notepad to display source code text. You can use any similar editor, including SideKick, PC Tools Deluxe editor, the Norton Commander editor or a number of other writing programs, including word processing programs that let you create simple ASCII files or text files without fancy formatting.

What Is The ANSI C Standard?

The C programming language has gone through all sorts of twists and turns during its development. This is not unusual for something involved with computer technology, and C programming is about as involved as you can get. It has, however, made it difficult to come up with a single implementation of the C programming language that can suit all readers of a book like this one.

As of this book's writing, there are all sorts of popular C language program packages on the market. Most of them are produced by Microsoft Corp. and Borland International. You can find a list of the more popular versions and their descriptions in Appendix D.

The version of C described in this book is called ANSI C or standard C. This is the version defined by the American National Standards Institute (ANSI) C Programming Language Committee X3J11. While the stated purpose of this committee was to "codify existing practice," it also standardized the basic features of the language.

Although none of the manufacturers of proprietary C compilers, (such as Borland International and Microsoft Corp.) claim to "support" the ANSI C standard, all their programs run standard C code and support the keywords and header files defined as part of the ANSI C standard. This might change over time, but all the examples in this book will run successfully after being compiled and linked by such C programming language packages as QuickC, Microsoft C, Turbo C++, and Turbo C Professional.

New Terms

One of the difficulties about learning something new, particularly an aspect of computer technology that can appear complex and arcane, is picking up the jargon. Most people have become familiar with such common terms as *CPU* (central processing unit) and *floppy disk* (a removable, flexible disk). Most computer users are familiar with such terms as *keyboard input* (what you type) and *display terminal* (your screen).

Terms that apply to programming, however, are most likely to be new to you. You should double-check the list of terms provided in Appendix C, along with their definitions, to make sure you understand C programming terminology the way I intend to describe it.

If you run across other terms in this book that you don't understand, you should probably read a DOS primer or computer textbook so you have a better idea of how your computer works.

xiv

Acknowledgments

I always have to remind myself that a computer book author deserves less than half the credit for any book that carries his or her name. (I hope that's not true just with my books.)

First, I'd like to thank Greg Croy, Acquisitions Editor at SAMS, for acquiring this book and being so patient throughout its development. Elementary books are often more difficult and painstaking to write than a more advanced treatment. Greg took great pains to make sure this book was developed successfully.

Next, I'd like to thank my editor, Kathy Carlyle, who shepherded the manuscript to final book form. A computer book editor with a sense of humor—and one who points out the parts she enjoys reading—is a valuable treasure. Kathy exhibited a grace under pressure that makes me believe she's going places. Watch out, Greg!

There's a crew of other people who took some responsibility in getting my manuscript to finished form: Greg Guntle, the tech editor, Susan Christophersen, the copy editor, and Ann Taylor, the formatter, all of whom helped make this book you're about to read.

Thank you all for your help.

Trademarks

All terms mentioned in this book that are known to be trademarks or service marks are listed below. In addition, terms suspected of being trademarks or service marks have been appropriately capitalized. SAMS cannot attest to the accuracy of this information. Use of a term in this book should not be regarded as affecting the validity of any trademark or service mark.

dBASE is a registered trademark of Ashton-Tate Corporation.

IBM, IBM PC, IBM PCAT, IBM PS/2, and PC DOS are registered trademarks of International Business Machines Incorporated.

Lotus 1-2-3 is a registered trademark of Lotus Development Corporation.

Microsoft, Microsoft Windows, Codeview, Quick C, and MS-DOS are registered trademarks of Microsoft Corporation.

Norton Utilities is a trademark of Symantec Corporation

PC Tools is a trademark of Central Point Software.

Borland C++, SideKick, and Turbo C++ are registered trademarks of Borland International, Inc.

Turbo Debugger is a registered trademark of Borland International, Inc.

WordPerfect is a registered trademark of WordPerfect Corporation.

XV

Getting Started

In This Chapter

If you've never written, compiled, and run a computer program before, this chapter is designed for you. First it describes the essential conditions of all computer programs. Then it goes on to describe the details required specifically for C programs.

What Is a Program?

A computer program, when created correctly, will execute from your DOS prompt and perform the action you've designed it to perform. For example, when you want to work with WordPerfect, you enter **WP** at your DOS prompt. Your computer loads the WordPerfect editor and displays the WordPerfect editing screen on your display terminal. After the WordPerfect program is fully loaded and you press a single character key, the character appears on-screen in your cursor location. When you press other keys, such as function keys or certain key combinations, other things will happen: You might spell check a document, display a list of your DOS files, or prepare to print a document. All these activities are controlled by the WordPerfect computer program (WP.EXE) that you've loaded into your computer's RAM.

When you exit WordPerfect, you remove the software program from your computer's memory. Your computer no longer responds to the same commands that it did when WP.EXE was loaded. You can type characters on your screen, but you can't do much more than that. You can't do more because the DOS operating system, which was loaded when you booted your computer, provides only a very primitive editor that takes over when WordPerfect disappears.

The WordPerfect software program combines several languages, but C and Assembler, the two most important programming languages for microcomputer applications, predominate.

The purpose of a computer language, like that of any language, is communication. In this case, you talk to a computer. More specifically, you tell a computer what to do.

If you've never written a computer program before, you should view computers as large, dumb animals that can work very quickly. A computer just does what you tell it to do. It does nothing on its own. The chief advantage of a computer is that it does almost anything you tell it to do, very quickly and usually without making a mistake—if your instructions are correct.

Because your computer will only do what you tell it to do, correct instructions are absolutely necessary. Your instructions must also be very specific. The burden is on you to insert the correct commands in the correct order. When you do, the computer does what you want it to do at the right time.

Writing a program with the correct instructions takes practice. As with any other language, you must start with a few common terms and repeat them frequently. Then you must combine them into a sentence that makes sense.

At its simplest level, a computer program is a sequence of instructions that tell your computer's CPU what to do. That, however, does not tell you how to write a computer program.

How to Create a Program

There are three steps for creating a computer program. The first step is to write the program correctly. The second step is to run the program and check its performance. The third step is to edit the program, correct errors, then run it again to double-check your work.

A more detailed look at each of these steps follows.

1. Type the correct commands in the proper sequence into an editor using familiar alphanumeric characters and numbers, then save the commands to a clean ASCII text disk file.
2. *Compile* the text file. This translates all the instructions you've typed into machine-readable code and saves them to a separate executable file. An executable file is one that runs under DOS—the sort of file you run when you load Lotus 1-2-3 or WordPerfect. (These files are actually called 123.EXE and WP.EXE, respectively, in which the EXE stands for "executable.")
3. Run the executable file.

Ideally, these three steps are enough. In reality, however, you must often take two more steps because a program usually doesn't work correctly the first time you run it.

4. First, find out what went wrong with the executable program, either by examining the incorrect results and figuring out the problem, or by debugging the program instruction-by-instruction.
5. Edit the program to correct the error or errors, then recompile the code and rerun the program.

Sometimes you'll need to repeat these last two steps several times to iron out all the bugs.

> ▶ **NOTE:** The term *bug* comes from the days when computers were driven by radio tubes. The heat and light from the tubes attracted insects, which shorted out the electrical connections. Although computers have come a long way since radio tubes, the term *bug* still refers to something that frustrates the successful operation of a computer.

These steps apply to all computer programs regardless of the language you use. The only step that concerns you when writing computer programs is step 1, typing the correct commands in the proper sequence. When you compile a program (step 2), the compiler does all the work. When you run the compiled program (step 3), your computer and the operating system do all the work. If there are any problems, you can follow step 4 and check them out.

3

(Step 5 is a collection of steps 1 through 3. Only the first part of step 5, editing the program code, concerns you.)

You can use a variety of languages to write computer programs, just as you can use a variety of languages to talk to people around the world. Fortunately, the range of computer language is much narrower than the range of human language. Some comparisons between human and computer languages are as follows:

1. You must use the correct words to get your meaning across. One word means one thing; another word means another thing. Human language allows more flexibility than computer language. For example, you can use the word *blue*, when speaking to someone, to mean a *color* or a *mood*. A computer, however, would understand only one meaning of a particular word.

2. In computer language, you must use the correct spelling for your words. You might understand *colour* to be the British variation of *color*, but your computer probably won't.

3. You must organize words in the order that makes the right meaning come across. *I love you* has an entirely different meaning when you rearrange it to *You love I*.

The comparisons just made can be summed up as three qualities that are common requirements for all computer programming languages: Correct commands, correct spelling, and correct syntax.

There are, of course, differences among the various program languages available, which brings us to the special characteristics of the C programming language.

What Is C?

The C programming language was designed by Dennis Ritchie in the early 1970s. Mr. Ritchie attempted to design a computer language that would be similar to how a computer works, but one that would require a shorter learning time for the programmer. C was an outgrowth of a language called B, which sprang from the first version called A.

The C programming language turned out to be quite successful, so that's where the development stopped (or more precisely, where it hovered.) Whereas C was originally designed for the UNIX version 5 operating system, it has been modified extensively for other versions of UNIX, and modified drastically to run in IBM PCs and compatible computers.

All this modification raised the cry for a standard version of the language. In 1983, the American National Standards Institute (ANSI) drew together a panel of computer professionals, who declared a version of C, called ANSI C, the standard. This is the version of C described in the book you're reading now.

▶ **NOTE:** C++ is the newest version of the C programming language. This version incorporates ANSI C, plus many other modern developments.

5

Where C Fits In

There are more than 30 years of history concerning the development of computer languages. Over time, however, three broad categories, or levels, of computer programming languages have developed. These levels are called high, middle, and low. The level is determined loosely by several characteristics.

A *low-level* language most nearly resembles the machine-readable code that results when the computer program is compiled. Assembly language is the best example of a low-level language, because each line of code approximates a single line of compiled code. This near 1:1 ratio is what makes programs written in assembly language run so fast. The negative side is that writing assembly language code is painstaking and tedious. Most of the work has to be done by the programmer. This is expensive in both time and money.

A *high-level* language is one that approximates the vernacular form of a spoken language. dBASE is a good example of a high-level language. Many dBASE commands are practically English language equivalents, and you're given lots of leeway about case (uppercase and lowercase) and syntax. This makes writing dBASE code fairly easy. But the code is so specific to the program (dBASE III PLUS or dBASE IV) that you can't run it under any other environment. This makes it expensive to move your operations to a different type of computer or operating system, or to work with a program other than dBASE.

Which brings us around to *middle-level* languages. These fall between low- and high-level languages, and generally retain the benefits of both. The C programming language is just such a middle-level language. On the one hand, you can use it to access low-level calls in your CPU (*central processing unit*—the microchip). On the other hand, you can use functions that access high-level calls to peripheral equipment, such as your disk drive.

The three chief advantages for programming in C are:

▶ You can learn the basics of the language fairly quickly.
▶ You can perform sophisticated operations in the programs you design.
▶ You can easily convert the programs for use on many different computer systems.

6

Although this is a somewhat superficial description of the C programming language, it should help you fit the language into the scheme of things.

How to Write C Code

The physical act of entering C code into a program is easy. If you've used a text editor or word processor before, then you've mastered the basic technique necessary for writing C code. All you do is type the correct commands in the correct sequence.

There are three things you need to remember when you write a computer program. Don't insert control characters except a tab mark or a hard carriage return. Pay close attention to the case of your commands. And arrange your command lines in some form of structure.

You can use any text editor or word processor that saves what are called "clean ASCII text files" to disk. This means you can enter all characters generally available on most IBM PC computer keyboards. This includes all the alphabetic characters (A to Z, a to z), all numeric characters (0 to 9), and all punctuation characters. The only thing you have to watch out for are control codes. Different programs use control codes in different ways, but your C compiler will most likely choke on any control codes it runs across. The only two you can use are the tab mark (^ I) created by pressing Tab, and the hard carriage return (^ J) created by pressing Enter.

If your C compiler program doesn't offer an editor, you might want to use a text editor you are familiar with. The PC Tools Notepad and the SideKick Notepad are examples of this type of program.

You also can use a word processor such as WordPerfect, Microsoft Word, or WordStar, if you don't insert special control codes. With some of these programs, you have to switch the mode the program uses when you want to save your text file to disk; for example, the nondocument mode in WordStar.

Regarding the use of case, the C programming language does process lowercase characters differently from uppercase characters. You'll have to make sure you enter a lowercase *a* when that's called for, and an uppercase *A* when that's called for. This differs from DOS, which treats both uppercase and lowercase characters identically. You'll find out more about the importance of case when you start to work with command terms and keywords.

7

When you write a C language program, even a small one, you'll find a style that makes writing your code, and making sense of the code you've written, much easier. This style is *structured code*, or code that has been modularly written. The code follows a structure so that you can make sense of its parts. It is *modular* in the sense that the clear structure lets you lift a section of the code out and insert it into another program.

For example, the following program is the first one you'll begin working with in the next chapter.

```
#include <stdio.h>
main()
{
printf("This is my first program!");
}
```

We won't dwell on the details here. You'll learn about them in the next chapter. What we're interested in are the five lines, each of which contains the six principal elements of a basic C program. These elements are:

Line 1   A header definition. In this case `#include <stdio.h>`.

Line 2   The function `main()`.

Line 3   The opening curly bracket (`{`).

Line 4   A program command, in this case `printf()`, and the text string it acts upon: `"This is my first program!"` surrounded by parentheses.

Line 4   The closing marker (`;`).

Line 5   The closing curly bracket (`}`).

You can insert more of these and other elements into a program, although you can have only one set of closing markers. But you must have at least one of each of these six elements in a program for it to work correctly.

This first example is arranged in an appropriate structured fashion. You could string some of these items together on the same line and the program would still run correctly. But if the program didn't run correctly, you would have to go back and edit one or more of the items, which means you'd have to dig around to find the mistake. If someone else had to dig through your code trying to make sense of it, they'd have an even harder time.

Here are two suggestions for ensuring clear and understandable programming:

1. Try to place each item in a program on a line of its own. For example, six items appear on five lines in the first example. You could move the closing marker (`;`) down to a line of its own, but this is an exception. It's considered more appropriate to place the closing marker after the last command.

2. Try to line up matching features in the same column. For example, the opening and closing curly braces are a matched pair, so they line up along the left margin. If you begin to use more groups that are surrounded by brackets, you might want to indent each group of opening and closing brackets so that the group reflects their ranking in the series.

With this sort of structured programming, it is easier to make sense of the items in the program. It is also easier to locate certain sections of the program, such as the header definition or the program commands, and to copy an item to another program if you want to use it another time.

8

If you find some of this information difficult to understand, don't worry. You'll begin working with many of these features in the next chapter. You'll start with hands-on training following the practice of memorizing a script, then putting it to use. This technique is described in the next section.

The Script Method

Learning to write a computer program language is similar to learning any other language. The best way is to use the language in simple situations, then develop your skill through increasingly complex situations. Studies have shown that learning a language by following a script is perhaps the easiest and most effective way to learn. We're going to apply this *script method* to your learning of the C programming language.

I'll describe what I mean by the *script method*. Here is an example of teaching someone who has just arrived in the United States (and who doesn't speak English) how to order a hamburger. First, you take him into a restaurant. You take a place in line and wait your turn at the counter. You say, "One hamburger" and wait until the cashier rings up the sale, at which time you are told how much you owe for the hamburger. You reach into your wallet, take out your money, and hand it to the teller. Perhaps you get some change back. Then you wait for the hamburger to arrive.

This is a very simple script, and millions of people perform it every day, almost exactly this way. It's impossible to order a hamburger any other way. You can't pay for it first, then say what you want to eat, then stand in line. You can't rearrange any of the key steps without taking the chance that you won't get your hamburger. So it is when you write a computer program. The steps must come in their turn, and they must be the right steps, or the program won't run the way you want it to.

9

Summary

In this chapter, you were introduced to the basic concept of programming and given some information about the C programming language in particular. For the rest of this book I'll take you through a variety of scripts that will help teach you the basic elements of writing C language programs. If you progress beyond the scope of this book, you'll still find yourself walking through the basic scripts just as I teach them to you each time you want to use one of the basic steps.

Chapter 2

Simple Program Output

In This Chapter

11

In this chapter, you'll learn about how a program generates information. This is where you write your first program, save it, compile it, then run it. After all that, we'll go back and take a closer look at the program by studying all the commands that make up the program.

What Is Input/Output

Basic input/output is the give-and-take between you and the computer. What you put into the computer is called *input*. What the computer gives back to you (or replies with) is called *output*.

The easiest way to get started with programming is to create a program that displays a simple message on your screen. This is the sort of program you'll create as your first lesson. This simple program will teach you how to design program output, or how your computer responds with output.

These five steps show you how to create your first program and all subsequent programs:

1. Open your editor and create the file you want to use. Make sure that you've logged onto the correct directory for saving your program text files.
2. Design the program by inserting the correct commands.
3. Save the program to disk.
4. Compile the program.
5. Run the program to see whether it works.

After you create your first program and watch it run, you'll modify the program to include more output from your computer. This will show you how easy it is to make the computer do the work for you.

12

Creating Your First C Program

The first thing to do when creating a program is to open the editor you're going to use. This is where you enter and save the commands that will be compiled to create the actual computer program.

> ▶ **NOTE:** You can use any text editor or word processor you want, as long as it saves what are called "clean ASCII text files." These are text files that contain alphanumeric ASCII characters only (A-Z, a-z, 0-9 and punctuation characters), and the tab and carriage return control codes. I prefer to use a text editor that can pop up and down over my DOS prompt. This lets me compile the program quickly and easily, run the program to check for bugs, then open the program again if I have to edit anything. I can make my changes, pop the program down again, recompile and rerun it, and so on.

For the examples in this book, I'm using the Notepad in PC Tools Deluxe Version 6.0, but many other text editors and word processors will work. From now on, I'll just refer to your "editor," as in, "Open your editor and type these commands" and "Close your editor and compile the program." It's up to you to follow the correct steps for opening the editor or word processor you use, inserting the right commands, and then saving the file and exiting the editor or word processor.

For your first program, open your editor and create a file called FIRST.C. Make sure that your current directory is the one containing your C program compiler. When your editor screen is showing, type the following text.

```
#include <stdio.h>
main()
{
printf ("This is your first program!");

}
```

These commands are called *source code* because they become the source of your program. The first step in all programming is to write correct source code. There are several specific and discrete parts to a source code file, but we'll back up and learn about them after you understand the complete process of designing C programs.

After you create the source code text file FIRST.C, you will take several additional steps before you can run the file as a program. These steps, which you will learn about shortly, are called *compiling* and *linking*. At this point, just be aware that the first step in C programming is to create correct source code. Everything else springs from that.

When you start writing the source code that comprises the FIRST.C program, make sure that you enter the text commands as you see them in this book. Each character should appear in its proper place and shape, as shown in Figure 2.1. Respect uppercase and lowercase spellings. No characters other than those that appear in the example should appear in your program.

When viewed on my screen, the program FIRST.C looks like Figure 2.1.

13

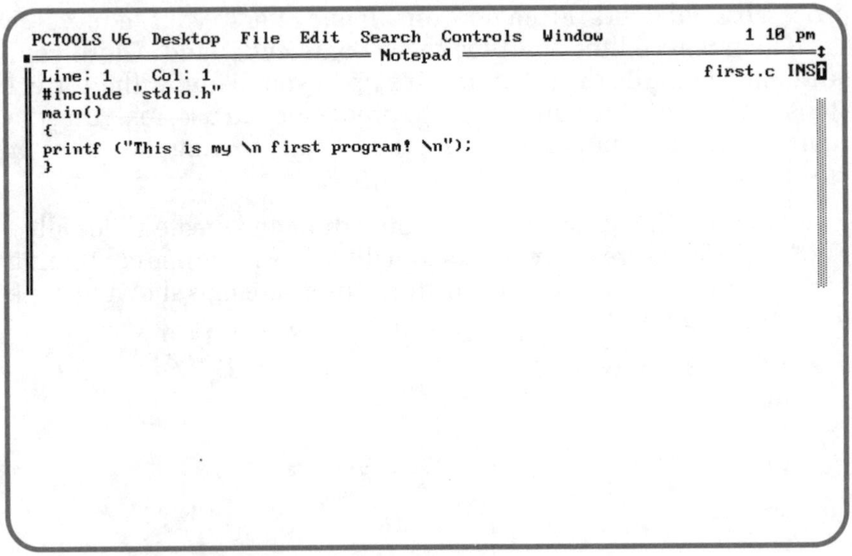

```
PCTOOLS V6  Desktop  File  Edit  Search  Controls  Window        1 10 pm
                                 Notepad
Line: 1     Col: 1                                           first.c INS
#include "stdio.h"
main()
{
printf ("This is my \n first program! \n");
}
```

14

Figure 2.1. Your first program viewed on screen.

Once you've typed all the commands in your first program, save the text file to disk. Make sure that it's saved with the file name FIRST.C. The name of a program is important for distinguishing it from other programs. The additional files you'll create by compiling and linking the source code file will automatically retain the file name you assign to the source code. You'll see how this works in just a moment.

If you're using a programming language package that lets you compile, link, and then run the program from your editor, do those steps now.

If you're using an editor separate from a C compiler, exit the editor now and compile, link and then run the program in that order. In case you're new to the practice of programming, the next several sections describe what happens when you compile, link, and run a C program.

What Is Compiling?

When you compile a source code text file, the compiler translates the language instructions you inserted (such as from Figure 2.1 above) into their equivalents in what is called *machine code*. Your computer can only understand machine code. It can't understand any other instructions. Therefore, to design a C program that runs on your computer, it must exist as machine code before it can run.

Machine code is read and processed directly by your computer's *instruction set* which is the heart of your computer's CPU—the part that processes all instructions. This part of your computer can read only whether an electrical charge exists. When a charge exists, it is given the value of 1. When a charge does not exist, the value 0 is given. Therefore, machine code consists of a series of 1s and 0s, called *binary bits*. You'll learn more about binary coding later in this book. For now, you just need to know that your computer can only understand binary bits—or machine code—and that your C compiler translates your source code instructions into matching binary bits.

Compiling a program is undoubtedly the easiest part of your programming work. Because compiling is so complicated, all the work is done by the compiler. The compiler is the major part of your C programming language package (Turbo C, QuickC, whatever). When you compile a source code file such as FIRST.C, you create what's called an *object file* using the same file name as the text file you're compiling. Therefore, when you compile FIRST.C, you end up with a file called FIRST.OBJ whose contents are shown in Figure 2.2.

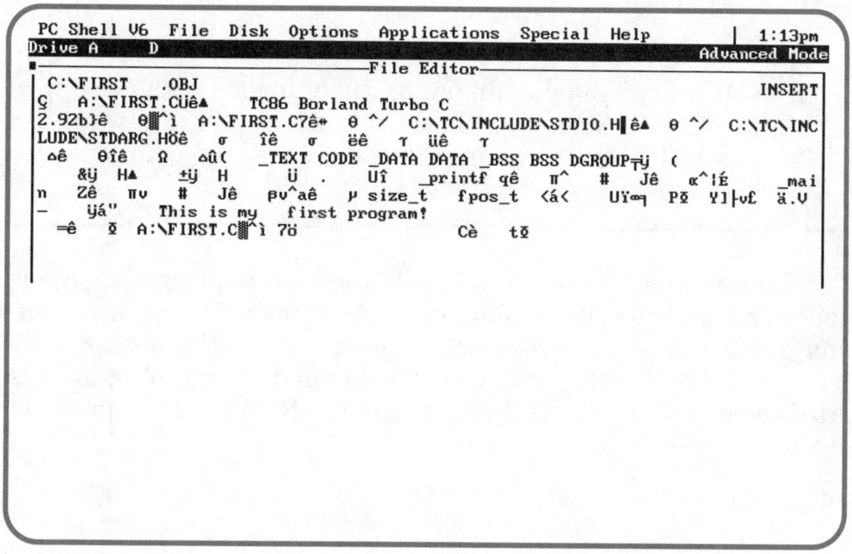

15

Figure 2.2. The contents of the top of FIRST.OBJ.

Don't spend too much time studying the internal contents of FIRST.OBJ. There's not much there that you can learn from. The purpose of the figure is to show you what a drastic change the compiler makes on the simple text file FIRST.C you saved to disk (see Figure 2.1).

When you compile a file, you may run across one or more warnings or errors. Warnings can usually be ignored, especially when you're starting out with small programs like the first examples in this book. If your compiler reports an error, jump ahead to the section in this chapter titled *Errors?*

After compiling a file successfully, the next step is to *link* the file.

What Is Linking?

Linking a file means taking the object file and linking the various functions you've inserted in the file to the function definitions in the specified header files. If linking works successfully, you create an *executable file*. This is a file that ends in the extension .EXE and can be executed in DOS. Notice that most of the application programs you load at your DOS prompt, such as WordPerfect (WP.EXE), Lotus 1-2-3 (123.EXE) and Microsoft Word (WORD.EXE), end with the .EXE file extension.

> ▶ **NOTE:** Some smaller programs can be loaded in DOS using the .COM extension. COM files are increasingly rare, whereas .EXE files are becoming more popular. A recent exception is Windows 3.0, which loads using WIN.COM.

Linking your C object files is just as easy as compiling the source code. The linker works automatically. As with compiling, however, you might run across some warnings or errors. Warnings can be ignored at this point. Errors *cannot* be ignored. If your program has errors, you need to correct them, then compile and link the program again.

If linking was successful, you should now have a file called FIRST.EXE. This is the executable file made out of your original text file FIRST.C that passed through the intermediate stage of FIRST.OBJ. Figure 2.3 shows the contents of the top of FIRST.EXE.

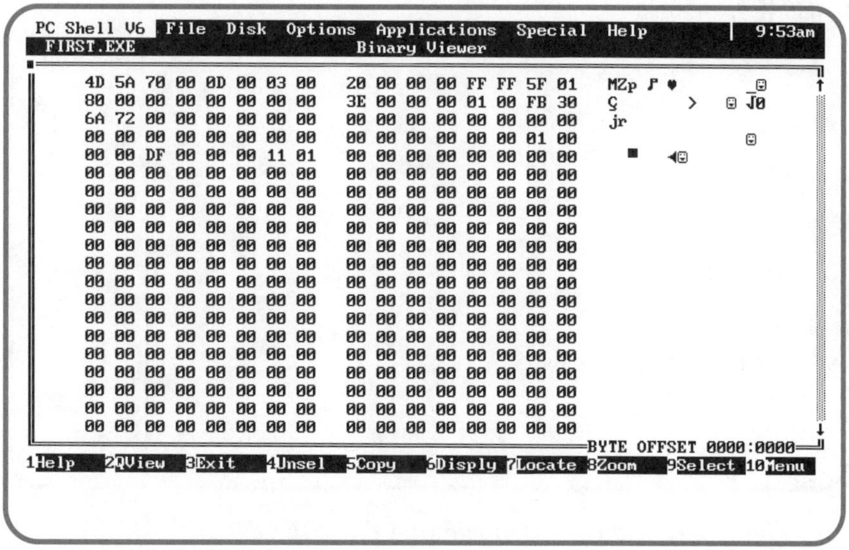

Figure 2.3. The contents of FIRST.EXE.

As with FIRST.OBJ, you can't make much sense out of these contents. The purpose of Figure 2.3 is to show how linking affects the development of your program file.

Running FIRST.EXE

To test whether FIRST.EXE does what you want, run the program. First, make sure that you're logged into the directory that contains FIRST.EXE.

Type **FIRST**.

You do not have to enter the file extension for an .EXE file.

Press Enter.

17

If all goes well, you should see the screen message shown in Figure 2.4.

```
C:\>first
This is my
 first program!

C:\>
```

Figure 2.4. The results of running FIRST.EXE.

The first line at the top of your screen shows the command you entered. The second line shows the results of running the program FIRST.EXE. When you run FIRST.C, the program places the string of characters "This is my first program" on your screen. This string of characters is called a *text string*. The third line down in Figure 2.4 shows that you've returned to the DOS prompt. FIRST.EXE was loaded, run successfully, and then emptied from DOS. The DOS system prompt shows that DOS has returned to control your computer.

> ⊘ **WARNING:** If your computer locks up while you are trying to run FIRST.EXE (or any other C language program), don't press Ctrl-C to break out of the program. And don't cold boot your computer by turning your computer off, then on again. Instead, warm boot your computer by pressing Ctrl-Alt-Del. This avoids the risk of corrupting data on your hard disk because the disk read/write head winds down without parking.

Once your first program FIRST.C works successfully, you can run it again several times. Each time you type **FIRST** and press Enter, DOS searches for a disk file called FIRST.EXE, reads the binary contents of the file, and does what the machine code tells it to.

> ▶ **NOTE:** When you want to run a program under DOS a second time, press F3 to reinsert the program name you already typed. For example, the first time you want to run FIRST.EXE, type **FIRST** and press Enter. After the program prints the text string and returns your DOS prompt, press F3 again, then Enter, and the program will run again.

Errors?

19

When you compile FIRST.C to get FIRST.OBJ, or when you link FIRST.OBJ to get FIRST.EXE, you might get error messages. If you do, find out what the error is and correct it. Your compiler should display some sort of error explanation or an error code that refers to a message describing the problem. With such a small and simple text file as FIRST.C, the only problem you can run across is a misspelled function or command. If this happens, go back and double check the contents of your version of FIRST.C, making sure that each word corresponds to the source code instructions for FIRST.C (as shown previously in Figure 2.1).

If you compile and link your first C program successfully, but the screen results you get are different from Figure 2.4, you should also go back and double-check the contents of FIRST.C.

Let's Back Up

Now that you've run your first program FIRST.C, you should understand the four elements that make up the basic structure of a C program. These four elements are as follows:

1. Declaring a header file.
2. Declaring the main() function.
3. Inserting matching curly braces.
4. Inserting one or more statements with functions defined in the declared header file or files.

You can do much more than this when you start creating sophisticated programs, but at the very least, you need to insert these four elements. In the rest of this chapter, we'll take a closer look at declaring the header file stdio.h, and inserting the main() function and the single statement that includes the printf function.

Figure 2.5 shows the source code for FIRST.C and points out the four elements.

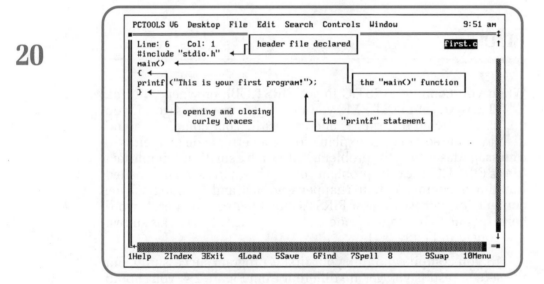

Figure 2.5. The four elements defined in FIRST.C.

Declaring Header Files

Header files are separate disk files that come as part of your C compiler. These files contain information that help your programs run. You must insert the name of a header file at the head of your source code programs when you want to use a function or command that's defined in the header file.

Functions are collections of commands that perform a specific task. The coding for these tasks is defined in the header file. To call on one of these tasks, you need only refer to the single name of the function assigned to the tasks, or commands. For example, the function printf prints the text that follows the function on your screen.

The definition for printf can be found in the header file stdio.h, which stands for *standard input and output header*. Because printing text is considered output, the printf function is aptly stored in this header file. Figure 2.6 shows the contents of the stdio.h header file in which the printf function is defined (this example is from Turbo C by Borland International).

```
PC Shell V6  File  Disk  Options  Applications  Special  Help     | 10:05am
Drive A  C                                                          Advanced Mode
                             ─File Editor─
  C:\TC\INCLUDE\STDIO    .H                                              INSERT
int       _Cdecl fprintf  (FILE *__stream, const char *__format, ...);
int       _Cdecl fputc    (int __c, FILE *__stream);
int       _Cdecl fputs    (const char *__s, FILE *__stream);
size_t    _Cdecl fread    (void *__ptr, size_t __size, size_t __n, FILE
*__stream);
FILE     *_Cdecl freopen  (const char *__path, const char *__mode, FILE
*__stream);
int       _Cdecl fscanf   (FILE *__stream, const char *__format, ...);
int       _Cdecl fseek    (FILE *__stream, long __offset, int __whence);
int       _Cdecl fsetpos  (FILE *__stream, const fpos_t *__pos);
long      _Cdecl ftell    (FILE *__stream);
size_t    _Cdecl fwrite   (const void *__ptr, size_t __size, size_t __n,
                           FILE *__stream);
char     *_Cdecl gets     (char *__s);
void      _Cdecl perror   (const char *__s);
int       _Cdecl printf   (const char *__format, ...);
int       _Cdecl puts     (const char *__s);
├┬┬┬┬┬┬┬┬┬┼┬┬┬┬┬┬┬┬┬┼┬┬┬┬┬┬┬┬┬┼┬┬┬┬┬┬┬┬┬┼┬┬┬┬┬┬┬┬┬┼┬┬┬┬┬┬┬┬┬┼┬┬┬┬┬┬┬┬┬┤
1        10        20        30        40        50        60        70

               Search Mode :    Search   Exit
```

Figure 2.6. The function printf *defined in STDIO.H.*

By placing the header file stdio.h at the beginning of your FIRST.C program, you can use all the functions contained within stdio.h, including printf. You're not required to use all the functions. You can use only one if you want to, such as the printf function.

Every C program must have at least one header file specified at the beginning of the program. Most C language compiler program packages provide an extensive library of header files, such as stdio.h, errno.h, and stdarg.h. Refer to Appendix C for a complete list of all header files contained within the ANSI C standard.

21

When you declare a header file you want to use, you must precede the header file name with the # symbol (press Shift-3). This symbol tells the compiler to process the text that follows during the first pass of the compiler. The compiler makes several passes when you compile a file. This gives the compiler a chance to verify all your instructions, sort them out, then match them up to declared header files—in a word, the compiler *digests* your source code and translates it successfully to the matching machine code instructions. The header file or files that contain functions you want to use in your program must be processed first, so the instructions that define the functions you use can be included in the machine code translation.

If the compiler finds any mistakes, it will log them on your screen as warnings (if they're relatively insignificant) or errors (if they choke the program and prevent it from working correctly). Most of your work designing successful C programs will be spent making sure that your source code goes through the compiler without any errors, and with as few warnings as possible.

22

You can use more than one header file in a program. You'll begin to use other header files as you become more adept with your C programming. You can imagine, however, that the header file `stdio.h` will become your most popular, because input and output are the most popular functions in C programming (indeed, in *all* programming).

For a complete list of header files that subscribe to the ANSI C standard, see Appendix C.

Declaring the main ( ) *Function*

Every C program source code file must contain the `main()` function, even if nothing else is specified for this first statement. The `main()` function marks the place where program execution begins. This is known as *making a call to* `main()`. Each line of code in a C program is processed sequentially. After calling `main()`, the next line of code is processed, and so on through all lines that you've inserted as the source code.

When all lines of code have been processed, the program first returns to `main()`, then unloads from your computer's memory.

There isn't much else you need to know about the `main()` function at this point except that it begins and ends all C programs.

You must always put `main()` at the beginning of the program, just before the first opening brace.

Inserting Curly Braces

Each function must contain its own pair of matching opening and closing curly braces. These braces mark off a *block*, or a set of logically connected statements assigned to a single function.

For example, the first `main()` function in FIRST.C is immediately followed by the opening curly brace. The block contains only one statement, the `printf` function and the text it handles. The closing curly brace follows this single statement and closes the block defined for `main()`.

When you begin to insert more than one function into your source code, you'll have to insert a matching pair of opening and closing braces for the block of statements assigned to each function.

23

Inserting Statements

The second function you used in your first FIRST.C program is `printf`. This function is actually part of a longer line called a *statement*. (There are several types of statements in C. We'll differentiate them when you begin to learn about the other types.) This type of statement contains a function and some additional information the function works upon. For example, the single command line statement in FIRST.C contains the `printf` function followed by the text that `printf` will print to your screen.

To use the `printf` function correctly, you must follow it with the characters you want to print surrounded by parentheses and quotation marks. You must also end the line with a feature called the *terminator*. This is the semicolon symbol. This type of terminator should come at the end of most lines in your C source code programs.

In your FIRST.C program, the characters to be printed by the `printf` function are

```
This is your first program!
```

You have to precede and follow the characters with quotation marks, and you have to place the entire character string including the quotes between a pair of parentheses (left and right paren, as editors call them).

In fact, we could refer to the `printf` function like this, `printf()`, as we referred to the `main()` function earlier. The only difference is that the `main()` function has to be included whether you add anything between the parentheses or not, whereas there's no need to use the `printf` function unless you specify some sort of text in the parentheses. Because the text will vary from one instance to the next, there's no need to specify the text when you refer to the generic `printf` command.

These are the rules for working with the `printf` function, but they don't apply to our work here.

Summary

24

In this chapter, you learned how to create your first C language program. You learned about the crucial five basic elements of every C language program: the header file, the `main()` function, the opening and closing curly braces, and statements.

If everything went swimmingly, you should dive into the next chapter. There we go into a little more detail about your first program and how you can enhance it.

Handling Input

In This Chapter

This chapter will introduce you to the concept of *input*. This is the information you put into the computer when you run a program that requires more information so it can finish its task.

You learned about basic output in the previous chapter. In this chapter, you'll learn how to handle basic input in your C source code programs.

What Is Input?

Input is what you put into your computer. It's the other half of the input/output procedure. You put things into your computer when you type characters from your keyboard and when you give commands by pressing function keys and multiple key combinations. You can also put things into your computer by pointing and clicking at objects with your mouse, or using some other input device such as a light pen or touch screen.

Input is a bit more complicated than output because your program must be ready to receive your input. Your program can't be doing other things when you try to give your computer some input. Your program should be prepared to recognize and use the information you put into the computer.

There are various ways of handling input, but the most popular and basic way is to use the scanf function.

The *scanf* Function

The scanf function stands for *scan function*. It is similar in design but not in function to the printf function. Whereas the printf function prints characters to some device (such as to your screen, as in the previous chapter), the scanf function is designed to receive characters from the keyboard.

The following steps occur when you run a C program that contains a correctly designed scanf function, and the scanf function is executed.

1. The first thing the scanf function does is instruct your computer to pause its execution and start scanning your input devices (in almost all cases your keyboard).
2. When data is received from your keyboard, the scanf function stores the information received up to the point where you press the Enter key.
3. The scanf function passes all the input back to your program.

The scanf function is a bit more demanding than printf. First, scanf requires that you define one or more variables before it is executed. You define variables using the INT keyword. Second, the scanf function definition must contain the format code %d as well as one or more of the variables you defined at INT to perform its work. Let's take a look at these requirements in practice.

26

Creating Your Second Program

The second program you will create is called AGE.C. This program will ask you how old you are. You'll reply with your age in years and the program will tell you how many months that equals. The source code for AGE.C is as follows:

```
#include <stdio.h>
main()
{
int years, months;
printf ("How old are you? ");
scanf ("%d", &years);
months = years * 12;
printf ("%d months", months);
}
```

Let's take a look at the parts of this program. First, you declare your basic input/output header file `stdio.h`, call the `main()` function, then insert your first curly brace. So far, this is identical to the first program, FIRST.C, that you created in the previous chapter.

The first line that follows the opening curly brace, `int years, months;`, is a new line that you probably don't understand. This is where you declare the two variables you're going to work with in this program. You declare the variables using the `int` keyword. In this case, `int years, months;` declares the two variables `years` and `months`. You can also declare each of the two variables on lines of their own, as follows:

27

```
int years;
int months;
```

Notice how each line must have a terminator, the semicolon. You don't have to change your version of AGE.C to include these two lines. This example is provided just to show you an acceptable alternative, which demonstrates how flexible you can be writing C source code. This alternative is, however, inefficient, because you use two lines when you need to use only one.

When you declare more than one variable using the `int` keyword, you're allowed to string the variables together as long as you separate each variable with a comma. Using the line `int years, months;` takes less time, less space, and is easier to understand.

The fifth line down should be easy to understand. This uses the printf function to print the text How old are you? on your screen. Note that a blank space has been inserted after the question mark. This blank space will be printed on screen right after the question. The blank space character is a character like any other. It separates the first character of your answer from the question mark so that the characters won't look squashed together on your screen.

The sixth line down in the AGE.C program provides the first example of using the scanf function. The syntax of the command—the way it is defined—should look familiar to you. It's similar to the way you define the printf function:

▶ Information specific to the scanf function follows the function name and is surrounded by parentheses.

▶ Part of the information inside the parentheses is bracketed by quotation marks.

▶ The end of the line contains a statement terminator, the semicolon.

Let's take a closer look at the information inside the parentheses. There are two parts to this information, each separated by a comma. The first part, "%d", is surrounded by quotation marks. This is called a *format code*, which is designed to read an integer (a whole number, such as 1, 2, 99, and so on) from the user and place it in the variable that follows.

The second part of the scanf information is &years. This is the variable that follows the format code. The variable years was declared earlier in the program using the keyword int. The symbol & precedes the variable to further define it.

The second part taken altogether defines the integer value received from the user (%d) as the value of years, or your age.

The seventh line below the scanf function definition in your AGE.C program performs a simple mathematical calculation, which you can probably recognize just by looking at it. The line months = years * 12 means that the variable months is equal to the value of years multiplied by 12. (The asterisk symbol [*] denotes multiplication in most computer programs.) There are 12 months in a year. The program takes your input, which is presumed to be your age in years, and calculates how many months the value is equal to.

The last line of code in AGE.C is a second simple `printf` function that prints the value calculated by the preceding line of code on your screen and follows the value with the word `months`.

Running AGE.C

You should now type in all the source code for AGE.C, save the file as AGE.C, then compile and link the program to create AGE.EXE. Once you've created AGE.EXE, run the program to make sure it works. At your DOS prompt:

Type **AGE**.

Press Enter.

Type **30**.

Press Enter.

29

Your screen should look like Figure 3.1.

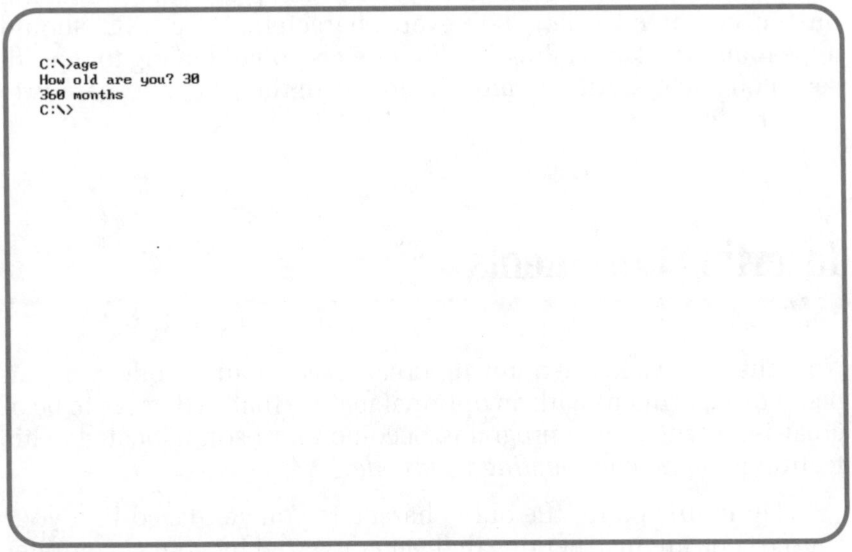

```
C:\>age
How old are you? 30
360 months
C:\>
```

Figure 3.1. The results of running AGE.EXE for 30 years.

Run the program again to notice some nuances. Type **AGE** and press Enter. Notice how the program pauses after displaying the question `How old are you?` You can find your cursor blinking one space to the right of the question mark. This reflects the empty space character you inserted after the question mark in your first `printf` function.

Now type your age (or any series of numbers). Don't press Enter yet. Notice how no calculation occurs. Each character you put into your computer is reflected on your screen. The program AGE.EXE continues to scan your keyboard and wait for another number.

Now press Enter to tell AGE.EXE that you've given it all the input you're going to give it. Almost immediately, the program replies with its answer, then returns you to your DOS prompt. Returning to the DOS prompt means that the program unloaded itself from your computer's memory and returned you to the operating system.

You might want to run this program several times to recognize all these fine points.

To run AGE.EXE again, just press F3. DOS remembers the last command you entered at the DOS prompt and places that command on the command line. The seven characters, AGE.EXE, should appear automatically. Pressing F3 relieves you of having to type all seven characters. All you have to do to run the program again is to press Enter.

Inserting Comments

Now that you've learned how to create basic source code, you can begin to experiment with an optional feature that will prove to be of great help when your programs become more sophisticated. This feature is called *commenting your code*.

Up to this point, the only characters you've placed into your source code are instructions that get converted by your C compiler to machine code. It's all been fairly straightforward, even if the

30

process hasn't always made sense. You copy the examples you see in this book, compile and link them, then try to run the executable file. If the file doesn't work, you go back and compare each line in your source code file with the example given in the book. Eventually, you get the program to run successfully.

As you create more source code files and fiddle with existing source code files, you'll find that you begin to forget what certain files do without running them. More disconcerting is the fact that, when you open a source code file to look at its contents, you aren't quite sure what certain commands do.

For example, if you were to take a quick look at the source code for AGE.C, you probably won't remember everything about it even though you learned all about it earlier in this chapter. You can imagine what it's like after you start creating lots of different programs, and much longer programs. You'll soon find yourself drawing a complete blank when you look at a file and wonder what it does.

31

This is the time to start adding comments. Comments are textual notes that describe or explain the program, or parts of the program. You insert comments as text on lines of their own in the source code file you write. Comments are not compiled as instructions when you create the executable program. You insert them simply for your own reference, or for reference to others who might look at your code and try to figure it out.

Text that forms comments is distinguished from other text by two symbols that precede and follow the text. A backslash followed by an asterisk (/*) precede the comments. Then an asterisk followed by the backslash (*/) follow the comments. These two pairs of symbols should surround text that serves as the comments as follows:

```
/* This is the text of some comments */
```

For the program AGE.C, you can add several comments that help describe the program. First, you can insert the name of the file AGE.C at the top of the source code. This helps you identify the file when you're working with it in an editor. Begin by viewing the contents of AGE.C on your display screen. Make sure that your cursor is at the top left corner of the file. Once you've positioned your cursor correctly, do the following:

Type /* **AGE.C** */.

Press Enter.

The second comment you should add is a description of what the program does. Make sure your cursor is on the second line of the program.

Type /* **This program converts your age in years to months** */.

Press Enter.

This second step should insert a blank line between the second comment and the header file declaration. Now save the file. The contents should look like the following:

```
/* AGE.C */
/* This program converts your age in years to months */

#include <stdio.h>
main()
{
int years, months;
printf ("How old are you? ");
scanf ("%d", &years);
months = years * 12;
printf ("%d months", months);
}
```

You can recompile this file, link it, and run it again if you want to. But because comments don't change the performance of the program (remember, they aren't converted into machine code by the compiler), you won't notice any difference in the way the program runs.

Although these first two examples of comments might seem trivial, they are good practice for your future work. We'll continue to add the name of each file and a brief description of what the file does to all our future programs. As our programs become more complicated, we'll insert comments between blocks of statements to describe what each block does. Well-commented programs are the sign of a good programmer at work, and there's no better time to develop the habits of good programming than when you start out.

Modifying AGE.C

You can modify AGE.C to calculate all sorts of matching values, as long as the matching values can be calculated one from the other. For example, you can calculate your age in days. In fact, you can modify AGE.C so that it calculates your age both in months and days and displays this information on screen. Let's do that now.

33

The following source code shows AGE.C after it has been modified to display your age in days.

```
/* AGE.C */
/* This program converts your age in years to days */

#include <stdio.h>
main()
{
int years, days;
printf ("How old are you? ");
scanf ("%d", &years);
days = years * 365;
printf ("%d days", days);
}
```

You should pay attention to the several changes you must make in this file.

▶ First, you should change the variable `months` to `days` as defined by the `int` keyword.

▶ Second, you should change the line that calculates the days so that `days = years * 365`, because there are 365 days in a year.

▶ Third, you should change the last line, the second `printf` function, and replace the two occurrence of `months` with `days`.

Now save, compile, and link AGE.C to create a revised version of AGE.EXE. When AGE.EXE has been created without errors, run the program.

Type **AGE.**

Press Enter.

Type **30.**

Press Enter.

34

When AGE.EXE displays the results, your screen should look like Figure 3.2.

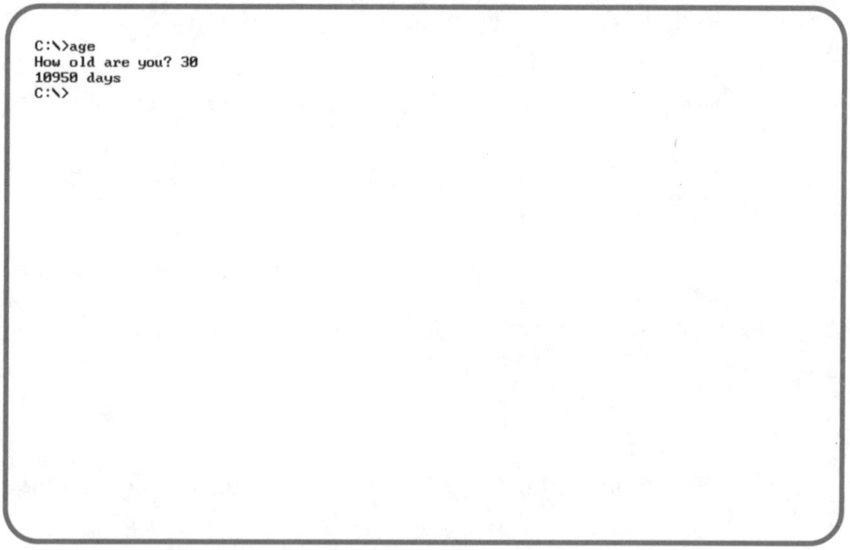

```
C:\>age
How old are you? 30
10950 days
C:\>
```

Figure 3.2. The results of running a modified AGE.EXE for 30 years.

You can try other values for calculating matching values, such as miles and kilometers (kilometers = miles * .6), pounds and ounces (ounces = pound * 16), and feet and inches (inches = feet * 12).

Mathematical Operators

You can also perform other simple mathematical calculations using other operators, such as the + symbol for addition, the – symbol for subtraction and the / symbol for division. All you need do is define the two variables correctly and define the method of calculation.

For example, you can use division to calculate your age in years from the number of months you've lived so far. We'll call this program MONYEAR.C, which stands for *months to years*. The source code for this file is as follows:

35

```
/* MONYEAR.C */
/* This program converts your age in months to years */

#include <stdio.h>
main()
{
int years, months;
printf ("How old are you? ");
scanf ("%d", &months);
years = months / 12;
printf ("%d years", years);
}
```

This program is similar to the first version of AGE.C except that the years are calculated from the months instead of the months being calculated from the years. Also, two lines of comments have been inserted at the top of the file.

Once you've written MONYEAR.C, saved the file to disk, and compiled and linked the program, you should run it.

Type **MONYEAR**.

Press Enter.

When the program asks your age in months, do the following:

Type **360**.

Press Enter.

Now try the results with a slightly different number of months.

Press F3.

Press Enter.

When the program asks your age in months, do the following:

Type **361**.

Press Enter.

Your screen results should be identical to those shown in Figure 3.3.

36

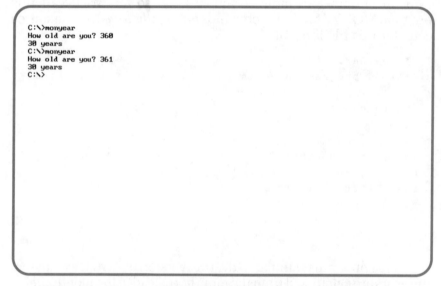

```
C:\>monyear
How old are you? 360
30 years
C:\>monyear
How old are you? 361
30 years
C:\>
```

Figure 3.3. Running MONYEAR for 360 and 361 months.

It's true that if you've lived 360 months, your age in years is 30. And it's also true that if you've lived 361 months, your age in years remains at 30. But the second calculation is not completely accurate. The number of months 361 divided by 12 yields the number 30.083333..., with a string of 3s extending out as far as you want to run the decimal point.

MONYEAR.EXE doesn't offer accuracy any more specific than in whole numbers, or integers. That's what the `int` keyword means: integer. The variables you're working with so far have been integers, or whole numbers. To test this limitation, enter characters that aren't integers (or numbers) when you're asked your age.

Press F3.

Press Enter.

Type **ABCDE**.

Press Enter.

You'll get a confusing answer, the exact nature of which depends on the C compiler you're using (Turbo C, Quick C, MASM, etc.). Let's try another series of non-integers.

Press F3.

Press Enter.

Type **XYX**.

Press Enter.

37

Again, you get a confusing answer. Your screen might look something like Figure 3.4.

```
C:\>monyear
How old are you? 360
30 years
C:\>monyear
How old are you? 361
30 years
C:\>monyear
How old are you? abcde
154 years
C:\>monyear
How old are you? xyz
154 years
C:\>
```

Figure 3.4. Results of using non-integer input with "int" variables.

If you enter any non-number values, you'll get this same answer. The program simply can't accommodate non-number values when performing calculations.

You can write a program that lets you experiment with subtraction by translating degrees from centigrade to Fahrenheit. This program also uses multiplication. Use the following source code for a file called CENTFAHR.C, which stands for changing centigrade temperature measurements to Fahrenheit:

```
/* CENTFAHR.C */
/* This program converts centigrade */
/* temperature to Fahrenheit */

#include <stdio.h>
main()
{
int centigrade, Fahrenheit;
printf ("How hot is it in centigrade? ");
scanf ("%d", &centigrade);
Fahrenheit = centigrade * 9 / 5 + 32;
printf ("%d Fahrenheit", Fahrenheit);
}
```

Notice how we place the comments that describe the program on two lines. You can insert all the comments you want in a program. It doesn't make the program work more slowly. Just make sure that you begin each line of comments with the /* combination of characters, and end the line with the */ combination of characters.

Once you've written and saved this code, compile and link the program to create CENTFAHR.EXE. Then run the program.

Type **CENTFAHR**.

Press Enter.

Type **0**.

Press Enter.

The answer displayed should be 32. Try another example.

Type **CENTFAHR**.

Press Enter.

Type **100**.

Press Enter.

Your screen should now look something like Figure 3.5.

38

```
C:\>centfahr
How hot is it in centigrade? 0
32 Fahrenheit
C:\>centfahr
How hot is it in centigrade? 100
212 Fahrenheit
C:\>
```

Figure 3.5. Results of running CENTFAHR.EXE for 0 and 100 degrees centigrade.

You can obtain a zero value for Fahrenheit if you enter **–11** for centigrade. You can obtain a minus value for Fahrenheit if you enter any value lower than **–19** for centigrade. Figure 3.6 shows the results of running these additional examples.

```
C:\>centfahr
How hot is it in centigrade? 0
32 Fahrenheit
C:\>centfahr
How hot is it in centigrade? 100
212 Fahrenheit
C:\>centfahr
How hot is it in centigrade? -18
0 Fahrenheit
C:\>centfahr
How hot is it in centigrade? -19
-2 Fahrenheit
C:\>
```

Figure 3.6. Running CENTFAHR.EXE for more examples.

As you can see, there are all sorts of calculations you can make using the four different mathematical operators +,-, *, and /. In later chapters, you'll learn how to make more precise calculations that allow for decimal numbers, as well as other types of calculations.

Summary

This chapter taught you how to "communicate" with a program while it is running. This lets you put information or data into a program, have the program process the data, then have it calculate a response based on the data. The concept of input is very important if you want your programs to do more than merely run through a programmed course of identical events each time the programs are run.

Variables, Functions, and Constants

In This Chapter

Computer programs use operators to manipulate variables and constants, which then form expressions. Variables can work inside or outside of functions, so the way functions work is important to understanding variables. This chapter describes variables and constants and how they work inside C programs.

You learned about operators in Chapter 3, when you practiced with simple input and mathematical calculations. In this chapter, you'll learn how these operators work with variables and constants.

What Is a Variable?

A variable is anything that can vary over time. Your age is a variable that changes with the passage of time. Although you can give your accurate age at any time, your age will increase as time goes by. Your weight is another variable that changes over time, although it can decrease as well as increase.

Variables in programming can change the same way. You use variables in programming to store values that can change and affect the results of your program.

C places a great deal of emphasis on variables, so you should spend time learning about them. You were introduced to the variables in Chapter 3 when you wrote your second program, AGE.C. You've used other variables since then, but only of the integer or `int` type. In this chapter you'll learn more about how variables work and how you can work with variables.

In C programming, you must declare a variable before you can use it. The basic syntax for a variable is as follows:

```
type identifier
```

There are five basic types of variables. There are three categories of variables. All five types fall into one of the three categories.

42

Types of Variables

The following are five basic types of variables, or data types, that you can use in the C programming language:

character These are designed to contain the 256 ASCII characters, such as 1, 2, 3, ..., A, B, C, ..., a, b, c, ..., and so on. You can also store the numbers 0 through 9 for small counts. This type of variable can contain characters up to eight bits wide, which allows for a total of 256 different characters.

integer These are designed to hold integers or whole numbers, such as 1, 2, 3, ..., 100, and so on. You cannot place numbers with decimal points in integer variables, only whole numbers. Most of the time, you will use these variables for counting purposes, such as the number of times a loop should be performed, or for cycling through a series of numbers. This type of variable can contain values up to 16 bits wide, which allows for a maximum of 65,535 numbers.

float These are designed to hold *floating point* numbers, or numbers with fractional parts or decimal points, such as 1.5, 3.14159 and 256,644.236799. The term *floating* *point* comes from the fact that the decimal point can move to a different location depending upon the result of the calculation. An example is, 2.5 x 2.5 = 6.25, in which the first two numbers contain a single decimal point number after the digit, whereas the calculation that results from multiplying the numbers results in a number containing two decimal points. The decimal point has *floated*. Float variables can contain values up to 32 bits wide, which allows for a maximum of over 1,000,000 numbers.

double   Similar to the float, these are designed to hold numbers with fractional parts or decimal points. The difference between this and the float-type variable is that double-type variables can store numbers up to 10 times larger than float-type variables. These types of variables are 64 bits wide, allowing for a maximum of 4 million numbers.

void   These do not return any values, hence the name *void*.

Table 4.1 lists the five basic types of C variables, their bit width, and the range of values they can contain.

Table 4.1. List of basic C variables.

Type	Abbreviation	Width	Range	Quantity
character	ch, chr	8	−128 to 127	256
integer	int	16	−32,768 to 32,767	65,535
float	f, balance	32	3.4E−38 to 3.4E+38	
double	d	64	1.7E−308 to 1.7E+308	
void		0	no value	

When you start out programming in C, you can refer to "data types" and "variables" as identical items. When you become more experienced, you'll find the differences are small, but important. Referring back to the basic syntax, you can declare these variables several ways, as follows:

```
int a, b, i;
char ch, chr;
float f, balance
double a;
```

Categories of Variables

Each of the five types of variables will fall into one of three categories depending on where the variable appears in the program.

Global variables   These appear outside any function and apply throughout the program, or *globally*. Usually, they appear at the beginning of a program, but they don't have to. They just have to appear outside any function.

Local variables   These are declared inside a single function. This makes the variable *local* to the function. The values assigned to local variables are lost after the function in which they are declared ends.

Formal variables   These are declared after a function name. They receive values passed to the function, but they can also behave like local variables.

44

Up to this point, you've used only local variables in your work with this book. That's because you've used only one function in each of the programs you've written, and you've placed the variables inside the single function. In this chapter, you'll learn more about functions, so you can use both local and global types of variables. You won't use formal variables for any of your work in this book.

You've also used only the integer, or int, type of variable in this book. This has let you work with whole numbers, such as 1, 2, 15, and 100, which are called integers.

Using Variables

You used variables in Chapter 3 when you wrote the source code for AGE.C, as follows:

```
#include <stdio.h>

main()
{
    int years, months;
    printf("How old are you? ");
        scanf("%d", &years);
```

```
        months = years * 12;

        printf("%d months", months);
    }
```

In this example, you used two integer type variables, `years` and `months`. You might want to run this program again to review how it works. It asks you a question, and you answer by typing your age. This number is accepted as the `years` variable. The number of years will vary each time the program is run, depending upon who answers the question.

AGE.EXE then performs a quick calculation converting your number of years to the equivalent value in months. The amount of months is assigned to the second variable `months`, which is then displayed on your screen. As with the number of years, the number of months will vary from one time that you run the program to another. These two examples illustrate how simple variables work within a program.

Variables can vary during the course of running a program, as you saw with the example of AGE.EXE.

You can also assign a value to a variable. The following example demonstrates assigning a value to a variable.

Type the following code into your editor, then link, compile, and run the program.

```
/* VALUE.C */
/* Demonstrates assigning a value to a variable */
#include <stdio.h>

main()
{
    int value1;
    int value2;
    int value3;

    value1 = 123;
    value2 = 456;
    value3 = 789;

    printf("This program prints the first value %d,\n", value1);
    printf("then the second value %d,\n", value2);
    printf("and then the third value %d,\n", value3); }
}
```

45

After saving this file to disk, link and compile the program, then run it.

Type **VALUE**.

Press Enter.

Your screen should look something like Figure 4.1.

```
C:\>value
This program prints the first value 123,
then the second value 456,
and then the third value 789,

C:\>
```

Figure 4.1. Results of running VALUE.EXE

As you can see, in the code for VALUE.C, first you declare the three integer type variables as value1, value2, and value3. Then you assign specific values to these variables. Finally, you include three printf statements that display the specific values you've assigned to the three variables on your screen. You probably won't assign specific values to variables too often, because variables are designed to contain information that varies due to the nature of your program.

To get a better understanding of variables, you should understand the difference between local and global variables. To do this, you need to understand the concept of *functions*.

Functions

Functions are the building blocks of C programs. Up to this point, you've worked only with programs that contain a single function, the `main()` function.

You use more than one function to divide your program into sections or blocks of code. Each function can serve as a single block. Each function should also serve a specific purpose. Functions let you control the flow of your program and determine which part of the program code will be executed next.

When you use more than one function in a program, you must refer to the next function to which you want to go. You must also separate the code of each function with its own opening and closing curly braces.

The basic format of a program that contains multiple functions is as follows:

47

```
main()
    function1()
    {
    function1() {
       statement1
       statement2
       .  .  .  .  .
    function2()
    }
    function2() {
       statement1
       statement2
       .  .  .  .  .
    function3()
    }
    function3() {
       statement1
       statement2
       .  .  .  .  .
    }
```

Notice that the code of each function is bracketed with its own set of opening and closing curly braces, including the `main()` function, which starts the program. Also notice that each subsequent function is called, or referred to, by the previous function. This reflects a linear or direct flow through all functions. `function1()` is called first, then `function()2`, then `function3()`, and so on.

You could also write the basic format as follows:

```
main()
      function2()
      {
      function1() {
        statement1
        statement2
        . . . . .
      function3()
      }
      function2() {
        statement1
        statement2
        . . . . .
      function1()
      }
      function3() {
        statement1
        statement2
        . . . . .
   }
```

In this case, `function2()` is called first, then `function1()`, then `function3()`. If you referred to one of the functions at the end of the section of code for `function3()`, you would end up with an endless loop, because the program would never finish.

In fact, just for the fun of it, why don't you copy the code for LOOP.C shown here, then compile and run the program. This demonstrates how an endless loop works.

```
/* LOOP.C */
/* Demonstrates an endless loop */

#include <stdio.h>
main()
{
```

48

```
  printf("This program demonstrates an endless loop\n");
function1();
}
function1() {
  printf("This is the first function\n");
function2();
}
function2() {
  printf("This is the second function\n");
function3();
}

function3() {
  printf("This is the third function\n");
function4();
}

function4() {
  printf("This is the fourth function\n");
function1();
}
```

49

Once you've saved this file to disk, compile and run it.

Type **LOOP**.

Press Enter.

The text messages displayed by the various `printf` statements in LOOP.C will begin to appear on your screen. You might or might not be able to read them, depending upon the strength of your eyesight and the speed of your computer. The messages will keep appearing until you break out of the program.

To break out of an endlessly looping program:

Press Ctrl-C.

Figure 4.2 shows what your screen should look like after breaking out.

If pressing Ctrl-C doesn't work:

Press Ctrl-Break.

```
This is the first function
This is the second function
This is the third function
This is the fourth function
This is the first function
This is the second function
This is the third function
This is the fourth function
This is the first function
This is the second function
This is the third function
This is the fourth function
This is the first function
This is the second function
This is the third function
This is the fourth function
This is the first function
This is the second function
This is the third function
This is the fourth function
This is the first function
This is the second function
^C

c:\>
```

Figure 4.2. Your screen after breaking out of LOOP.EXE.

The Break key is often labeled the Pause key, or Break shares some other key on your keyboard. If for some reason neither of these key combinations stops the endless loop:

Press Ctrl-Alt-Del.

This warm-boots your computer. If that doesn't work, you'll have to turn your computer off and then on again.

> ▶ **NOTE:** There are times when running a poorly written program can bollix your computer. Your computer might lock up, or your screen image might freeze. If this happens, walk through the above steps for breaking out of the endless loop.

Take a moment to go back and look closely at the code for LOOP.C. You might notice that the looping becomes endless after function4() performs. The last instruction in this function calls function1(). Each instruction beginning with the printf statement in function1() is called again in turn, and the loop is off and running.

Now that you have an idea of how functions help divide up sections of program code, you can use them to find out the difference in behavior between local and global variables.

Global and Local Variables

Earlier in this chapter, you learned some basic rules about variables. You can refine your use of variables by making some global and making others local. The difference in scope depends upon their range of action. Global variables remain the same throughout the entire program and operate globally. Local variables remain the same only within the function in which they are defined. Thus, they behave locally.

You can use a local variable over and over again, as long as you define it in each function of the program in which you want to use the variable. Once you've defined a global variable, it remains the same throughout your program.

51

The following program gives a good demonstration of how global and local variables work in a program. This program is a variation of the sort of calculations you made in the first programs you wrote for this book, such as AGE.C, MONYEAR.C, and CENTFAHR.C. Although we'll review instructions in this program after you run it, it might help to be aware beforehand that `int inch` defines a global variable, whereas `int feet` and `int yards` define local variables. The first is specific to `function1` and the second two are specific to `function2`.

```
/* VARIABLE.C */
/* Demonstrates the difference between */
/* global and local variables */
#include <stdio.h>

    int inch;

main()
{
    printf("This program converts yards and feet to inches.\n");
    function1();
    }
```

```
function1()
{
int feet;

printf("First calculate number of inches in feet\n");
printf("Enter number of feet: ");
   scanf("%d", &feet);

inch = feet * 12;

printf("%d inches", inch);
function2();
}

function2()
{

int yards;

printf("\n\nNow calculate number of inches in yards\n");
printf("Enter number of yards: ");
   scanf("%d", &yards);

inch = yards * 36;

printf("%d inches", inch);
printf("\nThat's all for now!");

}
```

Once you've written this code and saved it to disk and then linked and compiled the program, you should run it.

Type **VARIABLE**.

Press Enter.

The first part of the program displays the following information on your screen:

```
This program converts yards and feet to inches.
First calculate number of inches in feet
Enter number of feet:]
```

The first line contains information displayed by the very first `printf()` statement, which tells you what the program can do.

The second and third lines contain information displayed by the first and second `printf()` statements in `function1()`.

Type **40**.

Press Enter.

The program displays the following lines:

```
480 inches

Now calculate number of inches in yards
Enter number of yards:]
```

The 480 inches is 40 times 12, which is calculated by the following two lines of code in function1:

```
inch = feet * 12;
printf("%d inches", inch);
```

53

This is the first example of a local and global variable working together. The `feet` variable is local to `function1()`, but the `inch` variable is global to the program VARIABLE.EXE. You can see how it remains in effect through `function2()`.

Type **40**.

Press Enter.

The program displays the following four lines:

```
1440 inches
That's all for now!
C:\>
```

After running VARIABLE.EXE and giving the answers described in the preceding example, your screen should look something like Figure 4.3.

```
C:\>variable
This program converts yards and feet to inches.
First calculate number of inches in feet
Enter number of feet: 40
480 inches

Now calculate number of inches in yards
Enter number of yards: 40
1440 inches
That's all for now!
C:\>
```

54

Figure 4.3. Results of running VARIABLE.EXE.

Your DOS prompt might show a different path; that is, something like C:\TC\BIN> for Turbo C or C:\QUICKC\BIN> for QuickC.

With `function2()`, you calculated the inches from the yards you entered using the local variable `yards` declared in `function2()`, and the global variable `inch` declared at the beginning of the program.

Therefore, the global variable `inch` was used both in `function1()` and `function2()`, whereas the local variable `feet` was used only in `function1()` and the local variable `yards` was used only in `function2()`.

> ▶ **NOTE:** You can't design an example program similar to VARIABLE.C that runs on your computer and demonstrates how the local variable `yards` cannot be called in `function1()`, or how the local variable `feet` cannot be called in `function2()`.
>
> If you insert the appropriate lines of code that call on a variable inside a function that does not declare the variable, your C linker or compiler will give you an error, and no executable program file will be generated.

Modifiers

Variables can be modified certain ways for special needs. The four modifiers you can assign to variables are *signed*, *unsigned*, *long*, and *short*, although they don't all apply to all variable types. Table 4.2 shows their range of values and how they can be applied.

Table 4.2. Basic Modifiers for C Variables.

Type	Abbreviation	Bit Width	Range
character	char	8	−128 to 127
character	unsigned char	8	0 to 255
character	signed char	8	−128 to 127
integer	int	16	−32768 to 32767
integer	unsigned int	16	0 to 65535
integer	signed int	16	−32768 to 32767
integer	short int	8	−128 to 127
integer	unsigned short int	8	0 to 255
integer	signed short in	8	−128 to 127
integer	long int	32	−2147483648 to 2147483649
integer	signed long int	32	−2147483648 to 2147483649
integer	unsigned long in	32	0 to 4294967296
float	float	32	3.4E−38 to 3.4E+38
double	double	64	1.7E−308 to 1.7E+308
double	long double	80	3.4E−4932 to 1.1E+4932

As you can see, all four modifiers can be applied to integer variables. Because integers are used so often, you can simply use the terms *unsigned*, *short* and *long* without *integer*, or `int` following.

The *long* modifier can be applied to the `double` variable as well.

Constants

Constants are values that don't change during the course of running a program. Constants are distinguished this way from variables, which can change during a program run.

You can use four of the basic data types for constants that you can use for variables: integer, character, float, and double. As with variables, integer constants are for whole numbers, character constants are for displayable characters, float constants are for floating point numbers (numbers with fractional parts or decimal points), and double constants are for very large numbers.

There are three categories of constants you can use: string constants, backslash character constants, and notational or number constants. Now we'll take a closer look at each of these three categories of constants.

String Constants

A string constant is any group (or string) of characters. You must enclose string constants within double quotations, as follows: "This is a string of characters". You've been using this sort of constant since your very first program, FIRST.C, when you printed This is your first program to your screen. In fact, most of the printf() statements you've been using in this book include this type of constant.

In some cases, you have used the printf() statement along with the character format code "%c" or the decimal integer format code "%d" to display variables on-screen. You can use the string format code "%s" to display string constants. As an example, type the following code:

```
/* STRING.C */
/* Prints a string of characters on your screen */
#include <stdio.h>

main()
{
    printf("%s", "This is a string test.");
}
```

The "%s" format code is used more often for string variables, but this gives you an idea of how it works with string constants.

There are two other specific types of string constants for you to be familiar with: backslash characters and number constants.

Backslash Character Constants

Backslash character constants are used to emulate special characters and keys on your keyboard. Table 4.3 provides a list and brief description of 13 backslash character constants you can use when you write C programs.

Table 4.3. Backslash character constants.

Code	Meaning
\a	Alert
\b	Backspace
\f	Form feed
\n	New line
\r	Carriage return
\t	Horizontal tab
\v	Vertical tab
\x#	Hexadecimal constant (#=hex number)
\#	Octal constant (#=octal number)
\0	Null
\\	Backslash
\'	Single quote character
\"	Double quote character

57

These backslash character constants are also called *backslash codes*. You'll use the \n, \" and \' codes most often. The first inserts a new line, which helps format the printout, into whatever is being printed to your screen or the printer. The second two codes insert the double and single quotation characters into your text, which otherwise might be mistaken for required formatting. For example, to specify a character constant, you must surround the character with single quotations, whereas to specify a string constant, you have to surround the string with double quotations.

You should probably experiment with using backslash codes, so that you can visualize their effects on your work. As a first experiment, type the following code into your editor.

```
/* SLASH.C */
/* Demonstrates the effects of some */
/* of the backslash constant codes */
#include <stdio.h>

main()
{
    printf("This is a demonstration of the new line code.");
    printf("First new line\nSecond new line\nThird new line\n");
    printf("Fourth new line\nFifth new line\nSixth new line\n");

    printf("First we'll insert five single quotes \'\'\'\'\'\n");

    printf("Next we'll insert five double quotes \"\"\"\"\"\n");

    printf("Finally, we'll sound the alert five times \a\a\a\a\n");

    printf("That's all folks!\n\n\n");

}
```

After you save and compile this file, run it.

Type **SLASH**.

Press Enter.

Figure 4.4 shows the results.

You might want to reopen SLASHCOD.C and insert other backslash codes to see their effect.

The \N and \xN constants refer to the octal and hexadecimal display of numbers, which is explained in the next section and described in more detail in Chapter 9.

Notational Constants

Notational, or number, constants refer to alternative numbering systems used in the world of programming. You're familiar with the decimal system for numbering, which uses base 10. There are ten pennies in a dime, ten dimes in a dollar, and so on.

58

```
C:\>slashcod
This is a demonstration of the new line code.First new line
Second new line
Third new line
Fourth new line
Fifth new line
Sixth new line
Now we'll insert five single quotes '''''
Next we'll insert five double quotes """""
Finally, we'll sound the alert five times
That's all folks!


C:\>
```

Figure 4.4. Results of running SLASH.EXE.

59

The two other notational systems most often used in programming are called octal, which uses base 8, and hexadecimal, which uses base 16. The advantage of these systems is that their bases are powers of 2. Base 8 is 2^3, whereas base 16 is 2^4. The hexadecimal system is the most popular of the two because it can represent the highest value in the fewest number of digits.

Summary

In this chapter, you learned how operators work with variables and constants. You'll learn more about various notational systems in Chapter 9.

The ASCII Character Set

In This Chapter

In the previous chapters, you learned how to write simple C programs, then you learned about variables, functions, and constants.

In this chapter, you'll learn how to write a program that reaches into your computer and pulls out the ASCII character set, then displays it on-screen. This information will help you learn about the character-based display system used by most IBM PCs.

This information will help prepare you to learn about the programming notational system called hexadecimal, which you'll learn about in the next chapter.

What Is the ASCII Character Set?

The ASCII character set is a list of 256 characters, 255 of which can be displayed on a character-based computer display screen. The best way to understand the ASCII character set is to know the history of its development.

First, however, you should understand the importance of standards. Standards are necessary for most of the things we do in modern life. For example, you need to understand standard English to read this book you're holding in your hands. A better example might be the QWERTY typewriter keyboard. Among all the different kinds of typewriters produced in the world, from manual to electric typewriters, every English-language keyboard (and practically every foreign-language keyboard) is arranged the same way. The top row of keys contains numbers and punctuation marks, and the second row down begins with the six letters Q, W, E, R, T, Y—hence the name of the keyboard.

It wasn't always this way. When typewriters were first produced, many came out with their own arrangement of keys. This made switching from one typewriter to another very difficult. Typewriters became popular only after the QWERTY keyboard was accepted as the standard. People in greater numbers could be trained to use them, and typists could switch from one typewriter to another with little trouble, because they had to memorize only one layout of keys.

To demonstrate the enduring importance of a standard, you should realize that typewriters have been around for over 100 years, yet the QWERTY keyboard remains the standard. In fact, a more logical layout for keyboard keys has been devised but never accepted, certainly not as a standard. This alternative is called the "Dvorak" layout. On this keyboard the keys are arranged in such a way that the letters you use most often are grouped together close to your left and right forefingers. Letters you use less often are placed further away from your forefingers. The efficiency gained by using this keyboard is that you don't have to reach very far for the keys you use most often.

The QWERTY keyboard layout was designed with the width of the printing letters in mind. The solution was to place the fat and skinny keys in an alternating sequence (R is a fat key, T is a skinny key) so that the fat keys would not group together and jam the machine when you accidentally pressed two keys at the same time.

Although most typewriters are now electronic and fat keys versus skinny keys no longer matters, the QWERTY layout remains the standard and has even been adopted by computer keyboards.

Because computers are much more flexible than typewriters in displaying characters, a new standard had to be devised for the types of characters that could be displayed. This is the force that drove the design of the ASCII character set. It was designed by a committee of computer and engineering professionals whose purpose was to create a set of characters that all computer designers and users could work with as a standard.

The ASCII character set was created in 1963 and has gone through minor modifications. The first version contained 128 characters, and these remain unchanged today as the first 128 characters in the set. These include the 96 printing characters you'd use most often on a typewriter, such as the ten numerals 0 to 9, the 26 uppercase letters (A, B, C, and so on), the 26 lowercase letters (a, b, c, ...), and the 34 punctuation marks you're most likely to use (:;.,/). When you subtract 96 from 128, you're left with 32, which is the number of control codes in the ASCII Table.

You'll learn more about the details of the ASCII character set as soon as you learn how to write a program that displays the character set on your screen.

Your Third Program

The third program you'll write, called ASCII.C, will display some of the ASCII characters on your screen.

> ▶ **NOTE:** In most cases, certainly for computers in the United States, the ASCII character set will be the same as the U.S. character set. There are other character sets you can install using the DOS command COUNTRY, but you should refer to a DOS book to find out how to do this.

The character set you'll display on your screen won't be very pretty, but it will serve as a good way to show how simple programs can reach into the internals of your computer and pull out information stored there.

To create ASCII.C, type the following code into your editor, then save the file to disk.

```
/* ASCII.C */
/* Displays some ASCII characters on screen */
#include <stdio.h>

main()
{
    int display;

    display = 1;
      printf("%c", display);
    display = 2;
      printf("%c", display);
    display = 3;
      printf("%c", display);
    display = 4;
      printf("%c", display);
    display = 5;
      printf("%c", display);
    display = 6;
      printf("%c", display);
    display = 100;
      printf("%c", display);
    display = 101;
      printf("%c", display);
    display = 102;
      printf("%c", display);
    display = 103;
      printf("%c", display);
    display = 104;
      printf("%c", display);
    display = 105;
      printf("%c", display);
    display = 200;
      printf("%c", display);
    display = 201;
      printf("%c", display);
    display = 202;
      printf("%c", display);
    display = 203;
      printf("%c", display);
    display = 204;
      printf("%c", display);
    display = 205;
      printf("%c", display);
}
```

Once you've written this code and saved it to disk, compile the program and run it.

Type **ASCII**.

Press Enter.

If everything goes according to plan, your screen should look something like Figure 5.1.

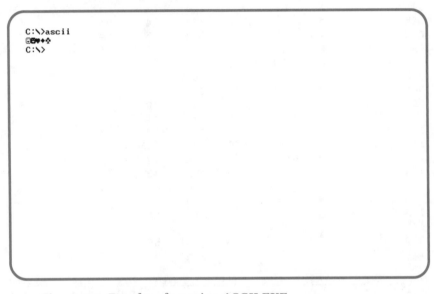

```
C:\>ascii
⌐○♥◄♦
C:\>
```

Figure 5.1. Results of running ASCII.EXE.

You might recognize some of the characters in this display, certainly the letter characters. Later in this book, you'll learn how to display most of the ASCII character set using many fewer commands. Table 5.1 shows the complete U.S. ASCII character set.

Table 5.1 shows each character, the decimal and hexadecimal value assigned to each character, and the code assigned to the first 32 ASCII characters.

Let's take a second look at the results of running ASCII.EXE.

Table 5.1. The complete U. S. ASCII character set.

Hex	Dec	Screen	Ctrl	Key	Hex	Dec	Screen	Ctrl	Key
00h	0		NUL	^@	1Ah	26	→	SUB	^Z
01h	1	☺	SOH	^A	1Bh	27	←	ESC	^[
02h	2	●	STX	^B	1Ch	28	∟	FS	^\
03h	3	♥	ETX	^C	1Dh	29	↔	GS	^]
04h	4	♦	EOT	^D	1Eh	30	▲	RS	^^
05h	5	♣	ENQ	^E	1Fh	31	▼	US	^_
06h	6	♠	ACK	^F	20h	32			
07h	7	•	BEL	^G	21h	33	!		
08h	8	◘	BS	^H	22h	34	"		
09h	9	○	HT	^I	23h	35	#		
0Ah	10	◙	LF	^J	24h	36	$		
0Bh	11	♂	VT	^K	25h	37	%		
0Ch	12	♀	FF	^L	26h	38	&		
0Dh	13	♪	CR	^M	27h	39	'		
0Eh	14	♫	SO	^N	28h	40	(		
0Fh	15	☼	SI	^O	29h	41	)		
10h	16	►	DLE	^P	2Ah	42	*		
11h	17	◄	DC1	^Q	2Bh	43	+		
12h	18	↕	DC2	^R	2Ch	44	,		
13h	19	‼	DC3	^S	2Dh	45	-		
14h	20	¶	DC4	^T	2Eh	46	.		
15h	21	§	NAK	^U	2Fh	47	/		
16h	22	▬	SYN	^V	30h	48	0		
17h	23	↨	ETB	^W	31h	49	1		
18h	24	↑	CAN	^X	32h	50	2		
19h	25	↓	EM	^Y	33h	51	3		

Hex	Dec	Screen	Hex	Dec	Screen	Hex	Dec	Screen
34h	52	4	62h	98	b	90h	144	É
35h	53	5	63h	99	c	91h	145	æ
36h	54	6	64h	100	d	92h	146	Æ
37h	55	7	65h	101	e	93h	147	ô
38h	56	8	66h	102	f	94h	148	ö
39h	57	9	67h	103	g	95h	149	ò
3Ah	58	:	68h	104	h	96h	150	û
3Bh	59	;	69h	105	i	97h	151	ù
3Ch	60	<	6Ah	106	j	98h	152	ÿ
3Dh	61	=	6Bh	107	k	99h	153	Ö
3Eh	62	>	6Ch	108	l	9Ah	154	Ü
3Fh	63	?	6Dh	109	m	9Bh	155	¢
40h	64	@	6Eh	110	n	9Ch	156	£
41h	65	A	6Fh	111	o	9Dh	157	¥
42h	66	B	70h	112	p	9Eh	158	₧
43h	67	C	71h	113	q	9Fh	159	ƒ
44h	68	D	72h	114	r	A0h	160	á
45h	69	E	73h	115	s	A1h	161	í
46h	70	F	74h	116	t	A2h	162	ó
47h	71	G	75h	117	u	A3h	163	ú
48h	72	H	76h	118	v	A4h	164	ñ

Hex	Dec	Screen	Hex	Dec	Screen	Hex	Dec	Screen
49h	73	I	77h	119	w	A5h	165	Ñ
4Ah	74	J	78h	120	x	A6h	166	a
4Bh	75	K	79h	121	y	A7h	167	o
4Ch	76	L	7Ah	122	z	A8h	168	¿
4Dh	77	M	7Bh	123	{	A9h	169	⌐
4Eh	78	N	7Ch	124	|	AAh	170	¬
4Fh	79	O	7Dh	125	}	ABh	171	½
50h	80	P	7Eh	126	~	ACh	172	¼
51h	81	Q	7Fh	127	Δ	ADh	173	¡
52h	82	R	80h	128	Ç	AEh	174	«
53h	83	S	81h	129	ü	AFh	175	»
54h	84	T	82h	130	é	B0h	176	░
55h	85	U	83h	131	â	B1h	177	▒
56h	86	V	84h	132	ä	B2h	178	▓
57h	87	W	85h	133	à	B3h	179	│
58h	88	X	86h	134	å	B4h	180	┤
59h	89	Y	87h	135	ç	B5h	181	╡
5Ah	90	Z	88h	136	ê	B6h	182	╢
5Bh	91	[	89h	137	ë	B7h	183	╖
5Ch	92	\	8Ah	138	è	B8h	184	╕
5Dh	93	]	8Bh	139	ï	B9h	185	╣
5Eh	94	^	8Ch	140	î	BAh	186	║
5Fh	95	_	8Dh	141	ì	BBh	187	╗
60h	96	`	8Eh	142	Ä	BCh	188	╝
61h	97	a	8Fh	143	Å	BDh	189	╜
BEh	190	╛	D4h	212	╘	EAh	234	Ω
BFh	191	┐	D5h	213	╒	EBh	235	δ
C0h	192	└	D6h	214	╓	ECh	236	∞
C1h	193	┴	D7h	215	╫	EDh	237	φ
C2h	194	┬	D8h	216	╪	EEh	238	∈
C3h	195	├	D9h	217	┘	EFh	239	∩
C4h	196	─	DAh	218	┌	F0h	240	≡
C5h	197	┼	DBh	219	█	F1h	241	±
C6h	198	╞	DCh	220	▄	F2h	242	≥
C7h	199	╟	DDh	221	▌	F3h	243	≤
C8h	200	╚	DEh	222	▐	F4h	244	⌠
C9h	201	╔	DFh	223	▀	F5h	245	⌡
CAh	202	╩	E0h	224	α	F6h	246	÷
CBh	203	╦	E1h	225	β	F7h	247	≈
CCh	204	╠	E2h	226	Γ	F8h	248	°
CDh	205	═	E3h	227	π	F9h	249	∙
CEh	206	╬	E4h	228	Σ	FAh	250	·
CFh	207	╧	E5h	229	σ	FBh	251	√
D0h	208	╨	E6h	230	µ	FCh	252	ⁿ
D1h	209	╤	E7h	231	τ	FDh	253	²
D2h	210	╥	E8h	232	Φ	FEh	254	■
D3h	211	╙	E9h	233	θ	FFh	255	

A Closer Look at ASCII.C

Understanding how ASCII.EXE works isn't too difficult if you take a closer look at the code you wrote to generate ASCII.EXE. The first five lines of code should look familiar to you. (For this example, we will count lines only when they contain a program statement.) They define the name and purpose of the file by using comments, then they declare the standard input/output header file `stdio.h` and `main()` function, and then they begin the body of code.

The sixth line declares the variable `display` to serve as an integer type variable. (We'll expand on variables towards the end of this chapter.) You'll notice as you scan the rest of the code that the `display` variable crops up in every `printf()` instruction. You'll see how this works as we explain the rest of the code.

The seventh line locates the symbol assigned to the ASCII character and assigns it to the `display` variable.

68

The eighth line prints the character currently assigned to the `display` variable to your screen. The first time this line of code is processed (`display = 1`), the first ASCII character is displayed.

From here on, you should view the code as matching pairs of instructions: the first instruction pulls out a character from the ASCII character set installed in your computer, and the second instruction prints the character to your screen. The `display` variable changes with each pair of instructions.

You can call up more ASCII characters by inserting more matching pairs of commands, but that seems like a lot of work. You'll find a much easier way to display more ASCII characters later in this book.

For now, you might experiment by substituting different numbers for the commands that already exist in ASCII.C. For example, display the characters for ASCII characters 150 through 160. You might find it easier to fiddle with this example of C code using a word processor that creates and saves clean ASCII files. This would let you search and replace for numbers quickly and easily.

Before we move on to other aspects of writing C code, let's take a look at control codes themselves, which are a subset of the ASCII character set.

What Are Control Codes?

Control codes are the first 32 characters in the ASCII character set. They get their name from the fact that each control character is designed to control some aspect of your computer and peripheral hardware, such as the printer and modem.

You can see how some of these characters control your computer when you run a shorter version of ASCII.EXE again. First copy ASCII.C to another file called ASCII1.C. You can do this using the DOS command COPY ASCII.C ASCII1.C, or you can use any of the popular DOS shells, such as Norton Commander, PC Tools Shell, or any program that lets you copy files.

Once you've created ASCII1.C, open the contents of the file in your editor. Remove all commands after the printf() statement that displays ASCII character 6. When you're finished removing these commands, the contents of ASCII1.C should be as follows:

69

```
/* ASCII1.C */
/* Displays some ASCII characters on screen */
#include "stdio.h"

main()
{
    int display;

    display = 1;
      printf("%c", display);
    display = 2;
      printf("%c", display);
    display = 3;
      printf("%c", display);
    display = 4;
      printf("%c", display);
    display = 5;
      printf("%c", display);
    display = 6;
      printf("%c", display);
}
```

Now save, compile, and run the program.

Type **ASCII1**.

Press Enter.

Your screen should change to look like Figure 5.2.

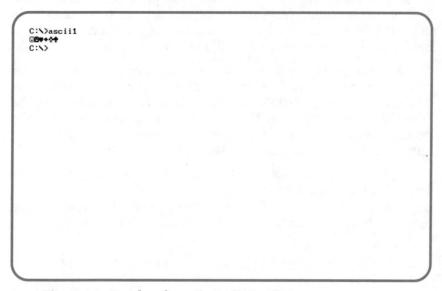

Figure 5.2. Results of running ASCII1.EXE.

What you see with this program are the first six characters of the ASCII character set. Nothing remarkable here. Let's try expanding our view of the ASCII character set. Insert the following two lines of instructions at the bottom of ASCII1.C.

```
display = 7;
   printf("%c", display);
```

Now save, compile, and run the program.

Type **ASCII1**.

Press Enter.

This time, instead of seeing a seventh character appear on your screen, you'll hear a bell. No visible character will appear. Run it a second time and watch closely.

Press F3.

Press Enter.

This time you might notice your cursor hang up for a moment after printing the sixth character to screen. Then you'll hear the beep. If you refer back to Table 5.1, you'll notice that the code assigned to the seventh ASCII character is BEL. This means bell. This control character sounds a bell.

Let's continue to expand our knowledge of the ASCII character set. In the program ASCII1.C, enter enough pairs of instructions to print all 32 ASCII characters. The contents of ASCII1.C should look like the following when you're finished:

```
/* ASCII1.C */
/* Displays some control characters on screen */
#include <stdio.h>

main()
{
    int display;

    display = 0;
      printf("%c", display);
    display = 1;
      printf("%c", display);
    display = 2;
      printf("%c", display);
    display = 3;
      printf("%c", display);
    display = 4;
      printf("%c", display);
    display = 5;
      printf("%c", display);
    display = 6;
      printf("%c", display);
    display = 7;
      printf("%c", display);
    display = 8;
      printf("%c", display);
    display = 9;
      printf("%c", display);
    display = 10;
      printf("%c", display);
    display = 11;
      printf("%c", display);
    display = 12;
      printf("%c", display);
```

```
      display = 13;
        printf("%c", display);
      display = 14;
        printf("%c", display);
      display = 15;
        printf("%c", display);
      display = 16;
        printf("%c", display);
      display = 17;
        printf("%c", display);
      display = 18;
        printf("%c", display);
      display = 19;
        printf("%c", display);
      display = 20;
        printf("%c", display);
      display = 21;
        printf("%c", display);
      display = 22;
        printf("%c", display);
      display = 23;
        printf("%c", display);
      display = 24;
        printf("%c", display);
      display = 25;
        printf("%c", display);
      display = 26;
        printf("%c", display);
      display = 27;
        printf("%c", display);
      display = 28;
        printf("%c", display);
      display = 29;
        printf("%c", display);
      display = 30;
        printf("%c", display);
      display = 31;
        printf("%c", display);
      display = 32;
        printf("%c", display);
  }
```

If this is too much for you to enter, just make sure that you enter enough instructions to display the ASCII characters in sequence from the first character through, say, character 15 or 16. Now when you save, compile, and run ASCII1.C, you'll get a display that looks something like Figure 5.3.

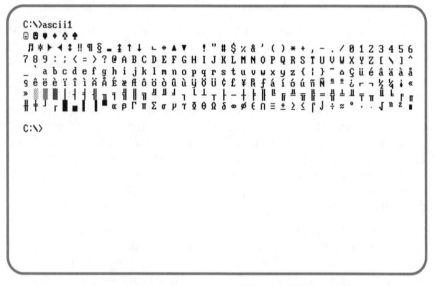

Figure 5.3. Results of running modified ASCII1.EXE.

Two interesting things happen. The first is that the characters stop printing on the first row, then resume printing on the second row. The second interesting thing that happens is that character 6, which appeared when you ran the previous version of ASCII1.EXE, no longer appears.

Let's take a closer look at this character display and find out the reasons for these events. If you refer to Table 5.1, you'll notice that the last character on the first line is a club (as in the "9 of clubs"), and the first character on the second line is a musical note. These two characters are, respectively, characters 5 and 14. All the other characters between them (6 through 13) don't show on the screen. Why is this? Well, you're seeing the effects of several control characters controlling your computer screen. Let's find out what's happening. Run ASCII1.EXE again and pay close attention to the first row of characters.

Press F3.

Press Enter.

Did you see a sixth character appear in the first row of characters, and then disappear? This was ASCII character 6, the spade character (as in "ace of spades") that you saw earlier. Run ASCII1.EXE again until you see this character appear and then disappear.

Why does it do this? You can tell from the codes assigned to the sixth, seventh, and eighth characters. The code for character 6, as shown in Table 5.1, is called ACK. This stands for *acknowledgment* and is used in communications to acknowledge certain things, such as the receipt of data transmitted to you by another computer. When you run ASCII.EXE, character 6 appears on your screen and remains there while the next character is processed. This next character is 7, which is called BEL. After the bell sounds, ASCII character 8 follows. This is called BS, which stands for backspace. When this appears, it causes your cursor to go backwards and erase the previous character, which is character 6. When you first ran ASCII1.EXE, it didn't display character 8, so no backspace character took effect.

In fact, the five control characters following number 8, that is, characters 9 through 13, control aspects that don't appear on your screen. Character 9 is a hard tab (HT), 10 is a line feed (LF), 11 is a vertical tab (VT) and 12 is form feed (FF). The line feed character moves your cursor down one line, but the next few characters still aren't displayed, so you don't know where your cursor is. The last character in the series of six nondisplayed control codes, character 13, serves as the carriage return (CR) and moves your cursor flush against the left margin. That's how the displayable control codes resume their appearance on the next line down and flush against the left margin as the sequence starts off with ASCII character 14.

This little detour should give you an idea of control codes and how they work. They aren't too important to C programmers, because you can control the behavior of your computer in other ways when you write C programs. But you should understand control codes if you want to understand the ASCII character set, which is important to you understanding you computer.

74

Summary

Control codes are the first 32 characters in the ASCII character set. They control various aspects of behavior in your computer equipment. For our work in this book, we're concerned only with the way control codes format and interpret output of your program to the screen or printer.

75

Chapter 6

Conditional Statements

In This Chapter

In this chapter, you'll learn how to expand your ability to program in C using the if conditional statement. The concept of conditional statements is important to programming. A conditional statement requires a condition to be met before something else occurs. Using conditional statements correctly lets you build programs that make some of the decisions themselves based upon certain conditions.

Conditional statements fall into the first of three broad types of statements you can use when writing programs in C. Conditional statements are a type of *selection* statement. The other two types of statements are called *iteration* statements and *jump* statements.

Learning how to use conditional statements correctly leads you into learning about the other types of statements, which are described in the next several chapters.

The *if* Statement

A conditional statement is one that proceeds in a certain manner depending upon the conditions. Conditional statements are called selection statements because they let your programs select what route to take. They insert a measure of judgment into your program and let the program "decide" whether to behave one way or another, depending upon a certain condition.

There are two types of conditional statements, if-then and if-then-else. As you can see, both begin with the command if, which is required for all conditional statements.

The first type of conditional statement is the simplest. This is the if-then statement. The command proceeds if a condition is true: *if* the condition is true, *then* something happens. The command does not proceed if the condition is false. In its simplest form, a conditional command can be expressed in the following format:

```
if (condition) statement
```

You specify the condition within the parentheses. You specify what will happen in the statement that follows the condition. The if command introduces the complete statement.

For example, you might want to write a program that calculates a paycheck, but only if that person has worked during the last pay period. If the database shows some time worked, then the pay is calculated; otherwise, no money is paid. You would write the command something like this:

```
if (work=yes) calculate pay
```

The preceding statement can be loosely interpreted as, "If the person has worked, then calculate the amount to be paid."

The second type of conditional statement builds on the first type but provides for an alternative action if the first condition is false. This is the if-then-else type of statement. This statement follows the usual if-then process if the condition is true. But if the condition is false, the statement follows another process specified by the else clause. It does not stop proceeding just because the first condition is false. The form for this statement is as follows:

```
if (condition) statement
     else (statement)
```

Using the paycheck example, you could generate a check if the person worked using the first statement. Otherwise (or, *else*) you could generate a letter saying no money was forthcoming using the second statement.

To see how these and other varieties of if statements work, let's look at some examples.

Your First Conditional Example

Your first conditional program will demonstrate how a simple conditional statement works with a number variable. Type the following code into your editor, then save the file to disk.

```
/* AGE.C */
/* Demonstrates the "if" condition statement */
#include <stdio.h>

main()
{
    int a;

    printf("Enter your age: ");
      scanf("%d", &a);

    if(a < 21) printf("You are a minor.");
}
```

79

None of the instructions in this code is new. You used all of them in the preceding chapter. After linking and compiling the program, however, we'll go back through each instruction so that you know how it works.

Once you've saved AGE.C, link and compile the program, then run it.

Type **AGE**.
Press Enter.

The first thing you should see is the request: Enter your age.

Type **2**.

Press Enter.

The program should display the reply: You are a minor. and return you to your DOS prompt. It has done its work and finished running.

To test whether the program AGE.EXE always gives you this answer regardless of your age, or whether it can differentiate between ages that qualify one as a minor, run the program a second time and give it a different answer.

Press F3.

Type **22**.

Press Enter.

The program should reply with nothing, but instead return you immediately to your DOS prompt, as shown in Figure 6.1.

```
C:\>age
Enter your age: 2
You are a minor.
C:\>age
Enter your age: 22

C:\>
```

Figure 6.1. Results of running AGE.EXE twice.

The program has taken your input and based its reply on the condition of your input, that is, whether your age is below 21.

Let's take a closer look at the code in AGE.C. The first six lines of code in AGE.C define the file name and purpose, declare the standard input/output header file and the `main()` function, and open the body of code. These are similar to the first six lines of code in your previous two programs.

The seventh line declares the integer variable `a`, which is similar to your second program.

The ninth and tenth lines are also similar to previous examples but deserve a little more explanation. The ninth line prints on your screen the request: `Enter your age:`. The tenth line receives the information you give through your keyboard and places it in the variable `a`.

The 12th line is the conditional statement. It analyzes the condition of the variable. If the variable (your age) is under 21, then your program will print `You are a minor` on your screen. If the variable is equal to or greater than 21, nothing happens and the program is finished.

In AGE.C, you use a new *operator* called `less than`. It's time now to take a closer look at the operators you can use in ANSI C.

81

Operators

Operators get their name from the fact that they perform operations on values. In the previous chapter, you used several simple arithmetic operators, such as `+` and `-`. These operators perform arithmetic operations on numbers.

There are four classes of operators you can use in ANSI C, providing a total of 17 individual operators. These operators are listed in Table 6.1.

Table 6.1. List of C operators.

Arithmetic Operators

Symbol	Name	Operation
+	Plus	Addition
–	Minus	Subtraction
*	Times	Multiplication
/	Slash	Division
%	Percent	Remainder after division

Increment/Decrement Operators

Symbol	Name	Operation
++	Increment	Increases the value
– –	Decrement	Decreases the value

Logical and Relational Operators

Symbol	Name
&&	And
¦ ¦	Or
==	Is equal to
!=	Is not equal to
>	Is greater than
<	Is less than
>=	Is greater than or equal to
<=	Is less than or equal to

Pointer Operators

Symbol	Name
&	The address of
*	The contents of the address

You'll see how each of these operators work in various examples throughout this book.

> ▶ **NOTE:** There is another category of operators called *bitwise* operators, but you won't need to know anything about these advanced operators for your work in this book or for elementary C programming.

Modifying AGE.C

Now that you know how AGE.C works, and you've learned a bit more about operators, you can modify AGE.C so that it performs a bit better for you.

The first modification will let you expand your use of operators. The second modification will let you learn how to write more compact code.

83

Your First Modification to AGE.C

You could improve AGE.EXE so that it makes a more thorough analysis by inserting one more conditional statement. This would display on your screen the message: You are not a minor. This message would appear whenever you enter a number equal to or greater than 21, thereby preventing what can be an abrupt ending if the program replies with nothing at all, but just returns you to the DOS prompt.

Insert the following conditional statement as the 13th and 14th lines of code in AGE.C:

```
if(a==21) printf("You are not a minor.");
if(a>21) printf("You are not a minor.");
```

The complete code should look like the following:

```
/* AGE.C */
/* Demonstrates the "if" condition statement */
#include <stdio.h>

main()
{
    int a;
```

```
        printf("Enter your age: ");
          scanf("%d", &a);

        if(a<21) printf("You are a minor.");
        if(a==21) printf("You are not a minor.");
        if(a>21) printf("You are not a minor.");
    }
```

Once you've saved this code to disk, link and compile the program, then run it.

Type **AGE**.

Press Enter.

Type **22**.

Press Enter.

This time the program should display the message: You are not a minor. You can experiment with higher and lower values, as well as the number 21, to see how well the program runs. Figure 6.2 shows the result of the previous example.

```
C:\>age
Enter your age: 22
You are not a minor.
C:\>
```

Figure 6.2. Examples for running modified AGE.EXE.

Your Second Modification to AGE.C

It's not always true that the most efficient code is the most reduced or compacted code, but you should always keep your eyes open for ways to reduce the amount of code you use.

For example, in our modified version of AGE.C, we have now inserted three conditional statements at the end that process your input for analysis. Because being a minor (below the age of 21) is an either/or condition—that is, either you are a minor or you aren't a minor—you should look for ways to make this analysis using only two conditional operators.

Take a look at Table 6.1 shown previously. Notice the logical operator >=, which is called *greater than or equal to*. You can use this operator in a single conditional statement to serve the work of the existing second two conditional statements. Once you've made this replacement, your code for AGE.C should look like the following:

```
/* AGE.C */
/* Demonstrates the "if" condition statement */
#include <stdio.h>

main()
{
    int a;

    printf("Enter your age: ");
      scanf("%d", &a);

    if(a<21) printf("You are a minor.");
    if(a>=21) printf("You are not a minor.");
}
```

85

Now when you save, link, compile, and run this program, you'll find you get the same results as when you previously ran the program. Removing the single line of code doesn't speed up the execution of the program noticeably, but it does make for more "elegant" code.

Your Second Conditional Example

You can write a conditional statement that's slightly more complex than AGE.C. The following program compares two numbers you give the program and then issues a reply based on the comparison.

```
/* NUMBERS.C */
/* Demonstrates the "if" conditions statement */
#include <stdio.h>

main()
{
    int a, b;

    printf("Enter your first number: ");
       scanf("%d", &a);
    printf("Enter your second number: ");
       scanf("%d", &b);

if(a < b) printf("The first number is less than the second.");
if(b < a) printf("The first number is greater than the second.");
}
```

Once you've saved NUMBERS.C, link and compile the program, then run it.

Type **NUMBERS**.
Press Enter.

The first thing you should see is the request: Enter your first number.

Type **4**.
Press Enter.

The program should now display the request: Enter your second number.

Type **3**.
Press Enter.

Now the program should display the following message: The first number is greater than the second. After that, you are returned to your DOS prompt. The program has finished running. Your screen should look something like Figure 6.3.

```
C:\>numbers
This program lets you compare two numbers
to see which one is larger.
Enter first number: 4
Enter second number: 3
First number is larger than second
C:\>
```

Figure 6.3. Results of running NUMBERS.EXE and answering questions.

87

But the limits of the program are still not exhausted. In fact, you haven't really seen the condition situation operate. Perhaps NUMBERS.EXE will always display the final message regardless of which numbers you put into the program. Let's run it a second time to find out.

Press F3.

Press Enter.

The program asks you to enter your first number.

Type **3**.

Press Enter.

The program asks you to enter your second number.

Type **4**.

Press Enter.

This time the program tells you that your first number is less than your second number. This demonstrates that, with an interior calculation, your input is processed sequentially by the two conditional statements.

A Closer Look at NUMBERS.C

The first six lines of code define the file name and purpose, declare the standard input/output header file and the main() function, and open the body of code.

The seventh line declares two integer variables, a and b. You'll learn more about other types of variables later in this chapter.

The ninth line prints the question asking for your first number. The tenth line takes your input and stores it in variable a.

The 11th line prints the question asking for your second number, and the 12th line takes your input and stores it in variable b.

You now have two numbers stored in two variables.

The 14th and 15th lines of code are two conditional statements that process the numbers in the variables. If the first is true, the message attached to the first is printed. If the first is not true, the program moves to the second conditional statement. If this one is true, the message attached to it is printed.

What happens if you enter the same value for both the first and second number? Try running the program that way.

Type **NUMBERS**.

Press Enter.

Type **4**.

Press Enter.

Type **4**.

Press Enter.

The program will give you no answer, but instead return you immediately to your DOS prompt.

Modifying NUMBERS.C

In the case of comparing two values, there are three possible results:

1. The first number can be less than the second.
2. The two numbers can be identical.
3. The first number can be more than the second.

You should probably include a conditional statement at the end of the program for each of the three possible conditions. In between the two existing conditional statements, you should insert this line:

```
if(a == b) printf("The two numbers are equal.");
```

The complete code for this modified version of AGE.C should look like the following:

```
/* NUMBERS.C */
/* Demonstrates the "if" conditions statement */
#include <stdio.h>

main()
{
  int a, b;

  printf("Enter your first number: ");
  scanf("%d", &a);
  printf("Enter your second number: ");
  scanf("%d", &b);

  if(a < b) printf("The first number is less than the second.");
  if(a == b) printf("The two numbers are equal.");
  if(b < a) printf("The first number is greater than the first.");
}
```

Now repeat the example for entering 4 as the first and second numbers, and you'll see the new message on your screen.

You can make more complicated conditional statements having the conditions take you in all sorts of directions. Before you tackle these types of examples, you should understand something about loops and what they can do, and how they rely on conditional statements. Loops are described in the next chapter.

The *if-then-else* Statement

Now that you know how to use the simple if-then statement, you should expand your exposure to if-then-else statements. As stated earlier in this chapter, the if-then-else statement uses the following syntax:

```
if (statement)
     else (statement)
```

A good example to start with would be to modify AGE.C. This is the program that tells you whether you're a minor. Because this is a simple binary condition (you are a minor or you are not a minor), you can get the same effect as the original program by replacing the last two lines of code with the following lines:

```
if(a < 21) printf("You are a minor");
     else printf ("You are not a minor");
```

The actual code should look like the following:

```
/* AGE.C */
/* Demonstrates the "if-then-else" statement */
#include <stdio.h>

main()
{

     int a

     printf("Enter your age: ");
       scanf("%d", &a);

     if(a < 21) printf("You are a minor.");
     else printf("You are not a minor.");
}
```

If the first condition is met, that is, your age is less than 21 (a < 21), the message You are a minor is printed on your screen. If the first condition is not met (age => 21), the second condition, which is preceded by else, will be carried out. This case prints the message You are not a minor.

You can nest if statements, or insert an if statement within another if statement, to enforce a condition within a condition. The syntax of this construction is as follows:

```
if (condition1) {
  if (condition2) statement2;
  if (condition3) statement3;
  else (condition4) statement4;
{
else statement1;
```

In this arrangement, if `condition1` is true, the statements nested under the `if (condition1)` statement will be processed in turn. If `condition2` is true, `statement2` will be processed, and that's the end of the program. If `condition2` is false, `condition3` will be processed. The program walks through `condition3` and `condition4` the same way. If all four conditions are false, then `statement1` will be processed.

This can seem pretty complicated without a specific example. Type the following code into your editor.

```
/* NEST.C */
/* Demonstrates nested if statements */
#include <stdio.h>

main()
{
    int a;

    printf("Enter your age: ");
      scanf("%d", &a);

    if(a<21){
      if(a<13) printf("You can't see any films
               without your parents' permission.");
      else if(a<17) printf("You can't see any
             X or R rated films.");
      else printf ("You can't see any X rated films.");
}
    else printf("You can see any film!");
}
```

91

Now save the code, compile it, and run the program.

Type **NEST**.
Press Enter.

Now try your age and press Enter. You should repeat this program by pressing F3, then Enter, then type another age, and finally press Enter to finish the program.

The first half of this program is identical to AGE.C. The nested `if` statement starts with the second group of commands.

You'll find conditional statements very useful throughout your programs. They're the first step towards building programs that make decisions for you.

The following chapters expand on your ability to build programs that do more work for you, and increasingly complex work.

Summary

In this chapter, you learned how to work with conditional statements. You designed programs that displayed output depending upon your input, or the condition of your input. You experimented with two example programs. The first program gave you an individual response depending upon a comparison of two numbers you put into a program.

There are four types of operations: arithmetic, increment/decrement, logical/relational, and pointer. This work prepares you for the next several chapters, where you will begin to work with loops.

Chapter 7

The *for* Loop

In This Chapter

This chapter introduces you to the concept of the *loop*. The loop is a technique that lets your programs cycle through a series of instructions instead of making a simple conditional decision.

Loops fall into the second category of statements called *iteration* statements. To iterate means to repeat; however, the term *repeat* usually means to go over something one more time. The term *iteration* implies frequent and insistent repetition.

There are three commands you can use to perform iteration statements: `for`, `while`, and `do-while`. This chapter introduces you to the `for` command and gives you examples of how you can use it. The next chapter will introduce you to the `while` and `do-while` commands.

What Is a Loop?

A loop is a graphic way to visualize the performance of an iteration statement. A group of commands are repeated—or iterated—within a circular process, which can be viewed as a loop. As long as your program continues to cycle repeatedly through the commands that comprise the loop, nothing else happens.

Cycling through a loop comes to an end when a certain condition is met. It's possible to design what's called an *endless loop*, or a loop that never completes cycling, but this type of loop is generally useless.

To understand the nature of loops more clearly, we'll start by taking a look at the for command.

The *for* Command

A for loop tells your computer to process the statement contained within the for statement depending upon three conditions. The basic syntax of the for statement looks like the following:

```
for (initialization; condition; increment) statement
```

The term *for* is the command. The term *statement* describes the process that occurs each time the condition proves true. There's little difference between the basic syntax of the for statement and the if statement, except when you take a look at the three terms within parentheses: initialization, condition, and increment.

They are described as follows:

initialization   This sets the initial value of the loop. In most cases, this will be the number 1, but it can vary depending on what you want to do with the loop and where you want it to start. As your computer cycles through each pass of the loop, this number is increased a certain amount depending on the *increment*, which is described shortly.

condition   This is some value that must be tested each time the loop repeats itself. It is the same thing as the *condition* that applies to the if conditional statement. As long as the condition remains true, the loop will process another cycle. As soon as the condition becomes false, the loop stops, and your computer proceeds to the next command in sequence.

increment This refers to the amount you want the value to increase with each pass of the program. Remember, as long as the condition remains true, the statement declared at the end of the for statement will be processed. The starting value is increased by the amount of the *increment* with each pass of the program.

These three elements must be surrounded as a group with opening and closing parentheses. Additionally, the first, second, and third elements must be separated from one another by semicolons.

As an example, if you set the initial value to 1, the condition as less than 11 (<11), and the increment to 1, the for loop will make ten passes. The statement would look something like this:

```
for (initial=1; condition<11; increment=1) statement;
```

On the first pass through the loop, the initial value is 1. Because this is less than the condition (11), the condition is true, the increment moves the value to 2 (1 + 1 = 2) and the statement is processed. During the second pass, the new value 2 is checked against the condition and found to be true again (2 is less than 11). The increment increases the value to 3, the statement is processed, and a third pass is made.

95

On the 11th cycle, the number 11 will be checked against the condition. Because 11 is not less than 11, the condition becomes false, and the loop is complete.

For another example, you can set the increment to 5 and leave the other two items unchanged, so the statement looks as follows:

```
for (initial=1; condition<11; increment=5) statement;
```

In this case, the loop will make only two passes because the increment has been set to 5. The first pass uses the initial value of 1, which is less than 11, so the statement is processed. The increment moves the value up to six (1 + 5 = 6), which is still less than 11, so the statement is processed a second time. The third pass moves the value to 11 (6 + 5 = 11), which proves the condition false (it's not less than 11). That's the end of the loop.

The best way to begin working with loops is to view how the for loop works with a counter. A *counter* is a concept. There is no code or device, as such, that does the actual counting. Each swing through the loops adds another number to the previous number, thus increasing the count with each pass through the loop. This counts numbers in sequence.

Your First *for* Loop Example

Your first example of working with the `for` statement will count numbers from 1 to 50, then display these numbers on your screen. Type the following code into your editor.

```
/* COUNT */
/* Displays the numbers 1 through 50 */
#include <stdio.h>

main()
{
    int number;

    for(number = 1; number <= 50, number = number+1);
    printf("%d ", number);

}
```

Once you've saved this file to disk and compiled it, run the program.

Type **COUNT**.
Press Enter.

Your screen should look something like Figure 7.1.

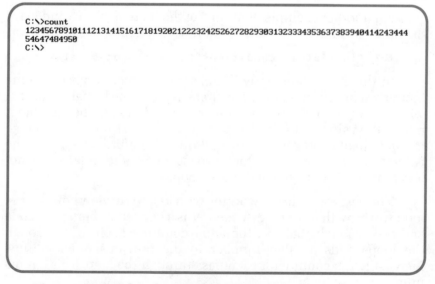

```
C:\>count
1234567891011121314151617181920212223242526272829303132333435363738394041424344
54647484950
C:\>
```

Figure 7.1. Results of running COUNT.EXE.

Fifty numbers appear in the sequence 1, 2, 3, and so on up to 50. This gives you two horizontal rows of numbers.

To understand the code in COUNT.C when compared to the basic syntax, you can run the two lines of instruction together, as follows:

```
for(number = 1; number <= 50, number = number+1); printf("%d ", number);
```

In this case, the variable we're using is an integer type called `number`. The initialization value, or initial value, `number = 1`, sets the initial value of the count to 1. You could set it at 0 or 2 or any other value that you want to use to begin the series of numbers.

Next, jump ahead to the third item, the increment `number = number + 1`. This increments, or increases, the count by a value of 1 each time the program reaches for the next value in sequence. You'll see how this works in the next paragraph.

Now jump back to the second item between the parentheses, the condition `number <= 50`. This sets the condition which, when met, forces the loop to stop. In this case, it sets the maximum value at 50.

The pass through the loop first displays the number 1, then increases the value of the number to 2 (1 + 1 = 2). The program compares the number 2 to the number 50. Because 2 is less than 50, the condition remains true (`<=50`), so the program displays the number 2, then increments the value to 3.

The loop continues to proceed this way by looping through the statement, incrementing the value, comparing it to the condition, then processing the statement, until the program gets to the number 50. Because 50 = 50, the condition remains true, so the number 50 is printed. The increment now moves the value to 51 (50 + 1), but when this is compared to the condition, the condition becomes false. That's when the loop stops, and you are returned to your DOS prompt.

You can display different numbers, and different combinations of numbers, by changing the initialization, condition, and increment values.

Modifying COUNT.C

Let's modify COUNT.C three ways so that it displays a different sequence of numbers. We'll do this by changing each of the three items that control looping: the initialization value, the condition, and the increment.

First, change the initialization value from 1 to 10. In place of `number = 1`, insert the value `number = 10`.

Second, change the condition from `number <= 50` to `number <= 1000`. This places the maximum value to be displayed at 1000.

Third, change the increment from `number = number+1` to `number = number+10`. This means that the numbers will increment in groups of 10, as follows: 10, 20, 30, and so on.

To make these changes, open COUNT.C in your editor and edit the code so that it looks like the following:

```
/* COUNT */
/* Displays the numbers 10 through 1000 */
#include <stdio.h>

main()
{
     int number;

     for(number = 10; number <= 1000, number = number+10);
     printf("%d ", number);
}
```

Make sure that you change the comments at the top of the file that define what the file does.

Once you've written and saved this code to disk, compile the program and run it.

Type **COUNT**.
Press Enter.

Your screen should change to look like Figure 7.2.

There are all sorts of variations you can use to display different sequences of numbers. You might want to play with a few examples of your own.

If you create a loop that keeps on running—an *endless loop*—you'll have to break out of the loop manually. Let's review the steps you learned previously for breaking out of an endless loop. First press Ctrl-C. If that doesn't work, press Ctrl-Break. If that doesn't work, press Ctrl-Alt-Del to warm-boot your computer.

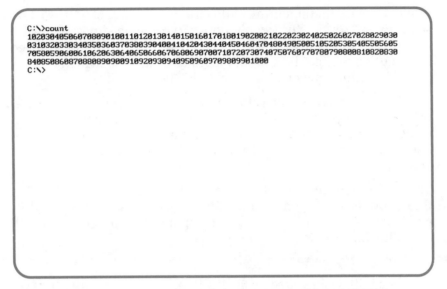

```
C:\>count
1020304050607080090100110120130140150160170180190200210220230240250260270280290030
0310320330340350360370380390400410420430440450460470480490500510520530540550560 5
705805906006106206306406506606706806907007107207307407507607707807900800810820830
84085086087088089009009109209309409509609709809901000
C:\>
```

Figure 7.2. Running the modified version of COUNT.EXE.

Incrementing and Decrementing

The terms *incrementing* and *decrementing* are fancy terms for common procedures. *Incrementing* means increasing the count, and *decrementing* means decreasing the count. Whenever you want to use specific sequences of numbers in your programs, as you've just done with COUNT.C, you'll find it easier to use the increment and decrement operators.

You experimented with a bit of incrementing in the previous example. First, you displayed every number from 1 to 50 (1, 2, 3, ...), then you displayed the numbers from 10 to 1000 using every 10th number (10, 20, ...).

You can also increase the value of a series of numbers, or increment the series, using the ++ operator. Rather than writing the increment value in the original version of COUNT.C, number = number+1, you could write the value as number++ or ++number. It doesn't make a difference whether the double pluses come before or after the variable name. The ++ operator combined with the variable name does the same thing as number = number+1, except that using the ++ operator is shorter and quicker. You might want to substitute this briefer form for incrementing in the original version of COUNT.C to see how it works. You won't notice the change in speed with COUNT.C. For the size of programs we're writing in this book, speed of execution will not be a problem, nor will it be changed much by any of the commands we can use at this level.

You can decrease the value of a series, or decrement the series, using the -- operator. In loop statements, the increment element can exist as an incrementer or a decrementer. Therefore, you can decrement the numbers in COUNT.C using the increment number--.

To see how decrementing works, edit the original COUNT.C so that it counts down from number 50 to 0 on your screen. To do this, replace the second-to-last line of code in the original COUNT.C with the following for statement loop:

```
for(number = 50; number >= 0, number--)    printf("%d ", number);
```

100

The initial value is set to 50, the final value (or condition) is set to 0, and the count goes backwards (it decrements).

Save and compile this program, then run it. You should get the same results as those shown in Figure 7.3.

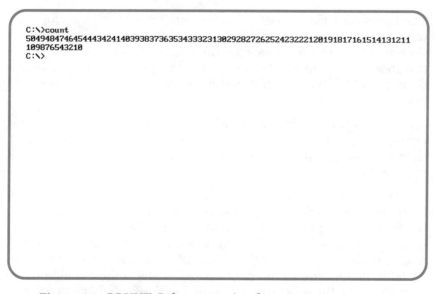

```
C:\>count
504948474645444342414039383736353433323130292827262524232221201918171615141
31211
109876543210
C:\>
```

Figure 7.3. COUNT.C decrementing from 50 to 0.

When you use the increment or decrement operators (++ or --), you can move through numbers only one by one. These operators add or subtract one number at a time, so you cannot use them, or modify them in any way, to increment or decrement by, say, groups of 10 numbers, as you did when you modified COUNT.C in the previous section of this chapter.

Your Second for *Loop Example*

You can also use the for statement to display a series of ASCII characters on your screen. The program you are about to write displays most of the set of characters.

To see how this works, enter the following code into your editor for a program called DISPCHAR.C.

```
/* DISPCHAR.C */
/* Display series of ASCII characters using a for loop */
#include <stdio.h>

main()
{
    unsigned char display;

    for(display = 1; display <= 254; display++)
    printf("%c ", display);
}
```

Once you've entered this code, save and compile it, then run the program.

Type **DISPCHAR**.
Press Enter.

Your screen should change to look something like Figure 7.4.

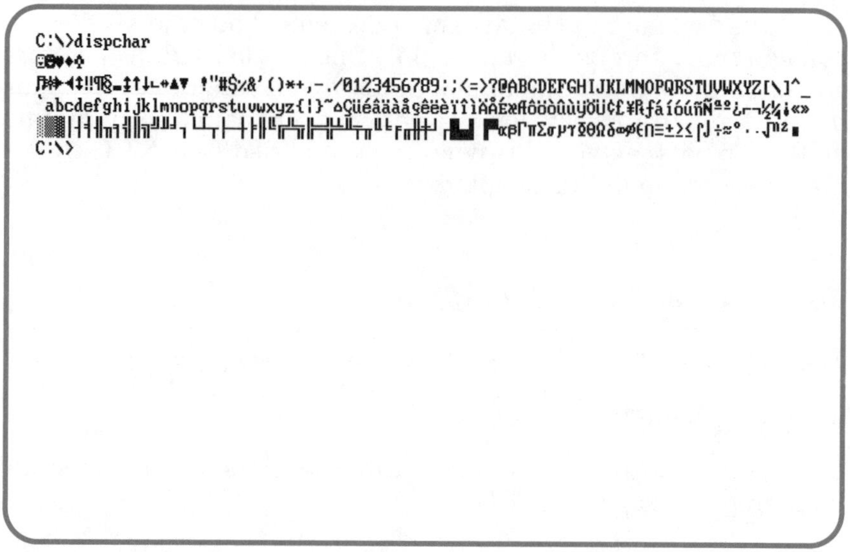

```
C:\>dispchar
☺☻♥◆♣
♠►◄‡‼¶§▬‡↑↓←�→▲▼ !"#$%&'()*+,-./0123456789:;<=>?@ABCDEFGHIJKLMNOPQRSTUVWXYZ[\]^_
`abcdefghijklmnopqrstuvwxyz{|}~⌂ÇüéâäàåçêëèïîìÄÅÉæÆôöòûùÿÖÜ¢£¥₧ƒáíóúñÑªº¿⌐¬½¼¡«»
▓▒░│┤╡╢╖╕╣║╗╝╜╛┐└┴┬├─┼╞╟╚╔╩╦╠═╬╧╨╤╥╙╘╒╓╫╪┘┌█▄▌▐▀αβΓπΣσµτΦΘΩδ∞φε∩≡±≥≤⌠⌡÷≈°∙·√ⁿ²■
C:\>
```

102

Figure 7.4. Results of running DISPCHAR.

The for loop in DISPCHAR cycles through the ASCII character set and displays each character in sequence. Actually, as described in Chapter 5, most but not all of the ASCII characters are displayed this way.

The 11 lines of code can be understood as follows. First, you should already be familiar with the first five lines. These define the file and open the main() function.

The seventh line of code declares an unsigned character variable called display. It must be a character-type variable because we want to display characters. It must also be unsigned because we want to display several hundred characters (see Table 5.1.)

The ninth and tenth lines are instructions for the for loop. Taking another look at the basic syntax, for (condition) statement;, we can see that the seventh line declares the three elements of the loop: (display=1; display=<254; display++), whereas the eighth line declares the statement printf("%c", display);.

The three elements of the for loop condition start by initializing the variable to start at character number 1, then setting the condition to become false when the 254th character is displayed, and finally incrementing the counter one character at a time. This for loop will print each character on your screen in sequence until the ASCII character is printed. Then the program will stop running.

Using Multiple Statements

You can use more than one statement with a single for loop if you want the loop to perform several instructions. You don't have to declare a second for loop for a second statement.

When you want to use more than one statement with a single for loop, list your statements according to the format for structured code. The basic syntax for a for loop with multiple statements follows:

```
for (condition) {
     statement1 ;
     statement2 ;
     statement3 ;
     statement# ;
     . . . . . ;

}
```

103

It's not necessary to place each statement on a line of its own. You could write the basic syntax as follows:

```
for (condition) {statement1; statement2; statement3; statement#; ...;}
```

The program would behave the same as if you had placed the statements on separate lines. But this style is harder to understand when you scan the written code and try to figure out what it means, or when you try to check for errors.

Using Multiple Header Files

You can use more than one header file in a program. Your work with the for loop gives us a good chance to introduce a second header file, MATH.H, that helps you perform numerical calculations. You'll learn about MATH.H by writing a new program called SQUARE.C.

We'll now use multiple statements and header files to design a program that calculates the square roots of decimal numbers from 1 to 10. This lets you use the for loop to perform real work.

Write the following code to a file called SQUARE.C.

```
/* SQUARE.C */
/* Displays the square root of decimal numbers from 1 to 100 */
#include <stdio.h>
#include "math.h"

main()
{
    int number;
    double square;

    for(number = 1; number < 100; number++) {
      square = sqrt((double) number);
      printf("%d %lf\n", number, square);
    }
}
```

104

We'll take a closer look at some of the new elements that appear in this file. For the moment, save the file to disk, compile it, then run the program.

Type **SQUARE**.
Press Enter.

Your screen should look like Figure 7.5.

```
77 8.774964
78 8.831761
79 8.888194
80 8.944272
81 9.000000
82 9.055385
83 9.110434
84 9.165151
85 9.219544
86 9.273618
87 9.327379
88 9.380832
89 9.433981
90 9.486833
91 9.539392
92 9.591663
93 9.643651
94 9.695360
95 9.746794
96 9.797959
97 9.848858
98 9.899495
99 9.949874

c:\>
```

Figure 7.5. Results of running SQUARE.EXE.

Now let's take a look at the new elements in SQUARE.C. The first three lines of code should look familiar. They identify and define the file and declare the first of two header files.

The fourth line includes a new header file called MATH.H. This contains a variety of mathematical operations that are useful in programming. Figure 7.6 shows part of the contents of the MATH.H file.

```
PCTOOLS V6  Desktop  File  Edit  Search  Controls  Window              10:37 am

Line: 1    Col: 1                                                    MATH.H INS↑
/* math.h

    Definitions for the math floating point package.

        Copyright (c) Borland International 1987,1988,1990
    All Rights Reserved.
*/
#if __STDC__
#define _Cdecl
#else
#define _Cdecl      cdecl
#endif

#ifndef __PAS__
#define _CType _Cdecl
#else
#define _CType pascal
#endif

#ifndef    MATH_H
←
1Help  2Index  3Exit  4Load  5Save  6Find  7Spell  8        9Swap  10Menu
```

Figure 7.6. Part of the contents of MATH.H.

You can see that the standard trigonometric functions, such as sine (`sin`), cosine (`cos`), and tangent (`tan`) are provided in this file, as well as other functions such as exponential (`exp`), log (`log`), and square root (`sqrt`). Declaring the MATH.H file by entering `#include "math.h"` is necessary in order to calculate the square root of numbers.

The fifth and sixth lines of the SQUARE.C program open the `main()` function.

The eighth and ninth lines declare two variables: the first an integer type called `number`, the second a double type called `square`. The first variable represents the decimal number, and the second variable represents the matching square root.

The 11th line of code introduces the `for` loop and defines the initialization value, condition, and increment of the three elements. Decimal numbers will begin with 1 and proceed through each integer to 100. An opening curly brace appears at the end of line 9.

105

This serves to compartmentalize the two lines of instructions that follow.

The 12th line introduces you to the `sqrt()` function. This calls on commands defining `sqrt()` in MATH.H and calculates the square root of the `number` variable, then places this value in the `square` variable.

The 13th line prints the current decimal number and its matching square root. The newline code `\n` ensures that each pair of decimal number and matching square root appears on a line of its own.

Summary

In this chapter, you were introduced to the concept of the loop and how to put it into practice. A loop in C programming must contain three elements: initialization, condition, and increment.

In this chapter, you worked with what's called a `for` loop. As you can see, the `for` loop is more complex than the `if` conditional statement. The `for` loop lets you cycle through specific conditions that perform a series of calculations and return results to variables.

The next chapter introduces you to two other types of iterative statements, the `do` loop and the `do-while` loop.

Chapter 8

The *while* and
do-while Loops

In This Chapter

107

In this chapter, you'll expand your knowledge of iteration statements by learning about the `while` loop and the `do-while` loops. Like the `for` loop, these loops process a statement based upon a condition. There are differences, however, in how these three types of loops operate.

In this chapter, we'll take a look at the `while` loop first. Next, we'll take a look at the `do-while` loop. This sounds like it should be similar to the `while` loop, but it operates in a different manner.

The *while* Loop

The `while` loop operates similarly to the `for` loop in that it performs a statement while a condition is true. The difference is that the `while` loop continues to operate while the condition is true, whereas the `for` loop operates once and then quits.

The basic syntax for the `while` loop is:

```
while (condition) { statement }
```

The statement is performed as long as the condition remains true. The loop stops performing when the condition becomes false. When this happens, the first instruction after the `while` loop is processed.

You should notice an important distinction between the basic syntax of the `while` loop and the `for` loop. Although the command, condition, and statement are all found in the same order, the statement for the `while` loop is surrounded by opening and closing brackets. The statement in the `for` loop is not surrounded by these brackets.

There are two things with which you need to be concerned. The first is creating a condition that's false from the beginning. When this happens, the loop won't perform.

The second thing you need to watch out for is creating a condition that can never be false. When this happens, the loop continues to cycle endlessly. You ran across an example of this in Chapter 4, when you wrote the program LOOP.C. There's no way out of an endless loop short of breaking out of your program. Your computer continues to cycle through the statements in the `while` loop forever. As you learned previously, you can sometimes break out of an endless loop by pressing Ctrl-C or Ctrl-Break. Otherwise, you'll have to *warm boot* your computer (press Ctrl-Alt-Del). Let's design some programs using examples of the `while` loop.

Your First *while* Loop

As a first example of working with the `while` loop, write a program that displays many of the characters in the ASCII character set. Enter the following code for CHARSET.C into your editor.

```
/* CHARSET.C */
/* Displays most of the ASCII */
/* character set on your screen */
#include <stdio.h>

main()
{

    char display;

    display = 1;
    while(display != 0) {
      printf("%c ", display);
      display = display+1;
    }
}
```

Save this code to disk, then compile and run the program.

Type **CHARSET**.

Press Enter.

109

Your screen should look something like Figure 8.1.

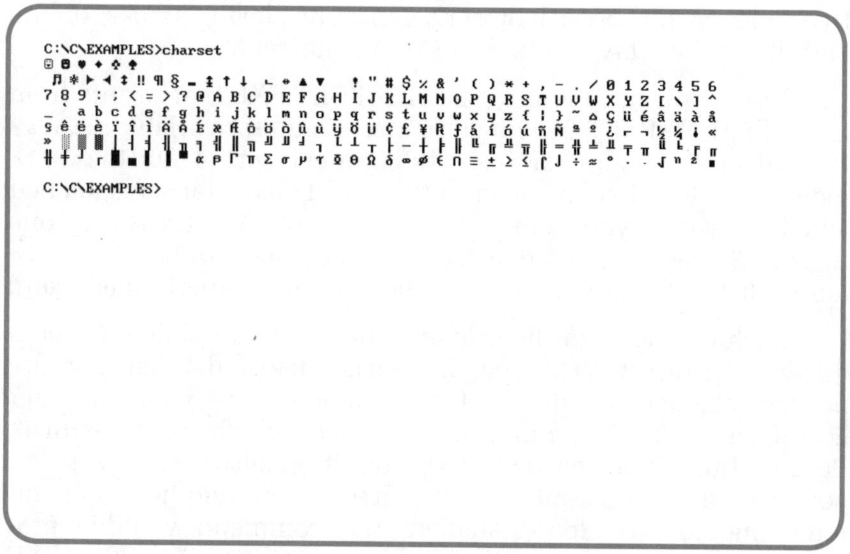

Figure 8.1. Results of running CHARSET.EXE.

You learned about the ASCII character set in Chapter 5. That's when you wrote ASCII.C to display several ASCII characters. Let's take a closer look at the code for CHARSET.C.

The first seven lines are fairly straightforward. They name and define the program, then open the `main()` function.

The ninth line declares a character variable called `display` (`char display`). We'll use this character variable to refer to the displayed characters.

The 11th line sets the counter for display at 1. This starts the first step for cycling through the ASCII character set.

The 12th line interests us the most. This is where the `while` loop starts. The instructions for the entire loop run through the 11th line. In this example, the condition is `display != 0`. Notice how an opening bracket appears directly after the condition.

The 13th and 14th lines define the statement as `printf("%c ", display) display=display+1`. The first part of this statement finds the character matching the counter number and displays it on-screen. The second part (`display = display+1`) adds one to the value of the display counter.

Notice how a closing bracket follows on the 15th line, effectively closing the `while` loop statement. The closing bracket on the 16th line effectively closes the `main()` statement.

When you run the program CHARSET.EXE that results from compiling CHARSET.C, your computer creates the variable `display` that will hold a single character. The counter is set to 1, and the `while` loop starts. The first character in the ASCII character set is fetched and displayed on your screen. Then the counter is increased by one digit to 2. Because this doesn't meet the condition of the `while` loop—that is, the number is not 0—the `while` loop is performed again.

Each character in the sequence of the ASCII character set is displayed in turn until the character set is exhausted. When there are no more characters to display (after character 256), your computer goes back to the beginning of the series, which begins with 0. Because this makes the `while` loop condition false (`display != 0`), your computer breaks out of the loop. If there were another command following the `while` loop statement, that command would be processed next. There is no other command, so the CHARSET.EXE stops and you are returned to your DOS prompt.

You can see another example of processing a `while` loop in FILL.C. This program inserts 24 text lines on your screen.

110

```
/* FILL.C */
/* Inserts 25 identical text lines on your screen */
#include <stdio.h>

main()
{

int line;

    line = 0;
    while(line != 24)
    {
       printf("\nThis is a screen line.");
       line = line+1;
    }
}
```

After you've written this file and saved it to disk, compile the program and run it.

Type **FILL**.

Press Enter.

You should end up with a screen in which 24 lines are filled with the text This is a screen line. The 25th line should display your DOS prompt, as shown in Figure 8.2.

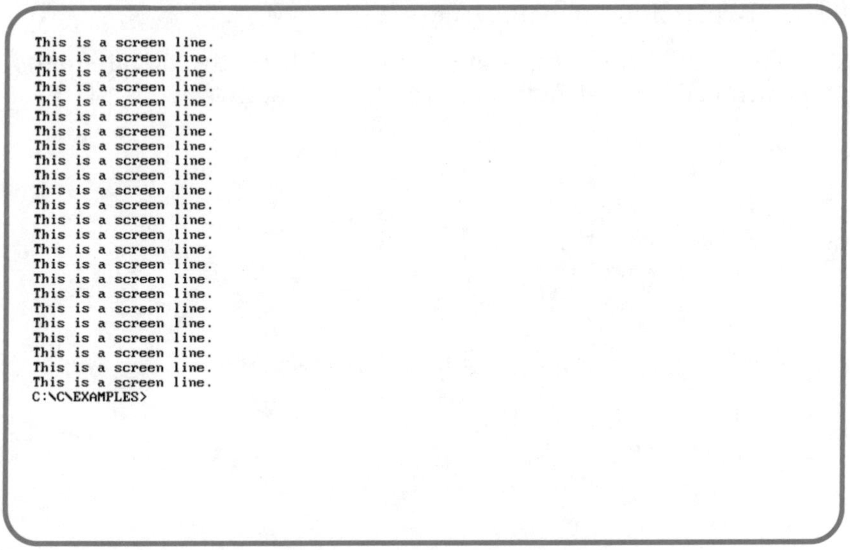

```
This is a screen line.
This is a screen line.
This is a screen line.
This is a screen line.
This is a screen line.
This is a screen line.
This is a screen line.
This is a screen line.
This is a screen line.
This is a screen line.
This is a screen line.
This is a screen line.
This is a screen line.
This is a screen line.
This is a screen line.
This is a screen line.
This is a screen line.
This is a screen line.
This is a screen line.
This is a screen line.
This is a screen line.
This is a screen line.
This is a screen line.
This is a screen line.
C:\C\EXAMPLES>
```

Figure 8.2. Results of running FILL.EXE.

In this case, the program defines an integer variable called `line`. The first line is set to 0 (`line = 0`). When the `while` loop starts, it inserts the specified text line (`This is a screen line.`) on the top line, using the `printf` statement. The line count is incremented after each pass through the `while` loop until line 24 is encountered. That's when this `while` loop terminates, leaving your cursor on the bottom line of the screen. You can position your cursor on different lines of the screen by changing the condition of the line count. Setting the condition to `while(line != 12)` will leave your cursor approximately in the middle of your screen.

You could modify FILL.C to clear your screen rather than fill it with lines of text. To do this, change the `printf` command as follows:

```
printf("\n");
```

This inserts a blank line on each screen line. Except for repositioning the DOS prompt at the bottom of your screen, this does the same thing as the DOS command `cls` (clear screen).

112

Multiple Statements

You can insert more than one statement in a `while` loop if you want. In this case, each statement will be performed in sequence as long as the `while` condition remains true.

The basic syntax for a `while` loop with multiple statements, when arranged in a structured format, is as follows:

```
while (condition) {
     statement1;
     statement2;
     statement3;
     statement#
     }
```

In fact, the general format for all `while` loops is

```
while (condition) {
     statement block
}
```

The statement block can consist of one or more statements. As is true with all while loops, the statement—or in this case, group of statements—is surrounded by opening and closing brackets. When your computer runs across such a while loop and the condition remains true, each statement is processed in turn: first statement1, then statement2, and so on through all statements in the list. When the last statement is processed, your computer goes back to the top of the loop and checks the condition. If it remains true, the program runs through the series of multiple statements again in sequence. If the condition has become false, the loop is overlooked and the first instruction that follows the while loop statements is processed next.

As an example, the following program, DECASCII.C, displays the decimal value assigned to any ASCII character you specify.

```
/* DECASCII.C */
/* Prints the decimal value of the
/* requested ASCII character */
#include <stdio.h>

main()
{

char display, oncemore;

    oncemore = '1';
    while(oncemore == '1') {
        printf("\nTell me the ASCII decimal value of this character: ");
        scanf("\n%c",&display);
        printf("\nThe ASCII value of \"%c\" is %d\n",display,display);
        printf("\nPress [1], then [Enter] to check another character ");
        printf("\nType any other character, then press [Enter] ");
        printf("\nto exit the program: ");
        scanf("\n%c",&oncemore);
    }
}
```

113

This while loop contains a series of seven printf and scanf statements, which comprise the statement block or series of while loop statements.

To see how the program works, save the file to disk, then compile and run it. We'll walk through the operation of the program.

Type **DECASCII**.
Press Enter.

You will be asked to enter a character using the question in your first `printf` statement. This can be any character on your keyboard. For example:

Type **U**. *This means press Shift-U to insert an uppercase U.*
Press Enter.

This enters the character into the `display` variable. The next line of the program takes the character you've typed (`%c`), in this case, u, and displays it on-screen between quotation marks, then converts it to its equivalent decimal value (`%d`) and displays this value on-screen.

Next the program asks whether you want to find the decimal equivalent of another character or to exit the program. I've selected the 1 key as your choice to continue, because you can press it easily with your left hand and press Enter with your right hand. At this point in the program, your screen should look like Figure 8.3.

114

```
C:\C\EXAMPLES>decascii

Tell me the ASCII decimal value of this character: U

The ASCII value of "U" is 85

Press [1], then [Enter] to check another character
Type any other character, then press [Enter]
to exit the program:
```

Figure 8.3. Results of partially running DECASCII.EXE.

To continue checking another character, press **1**, then Enter. The 1 character has been assigned to the variable `oncemore` (`oncemore = '1'`). When you enter a character into the `oncemore` variable using the final `scanf` statement, the condition remains true if you press 1, and becomes false if you enter any other character. If the condition remains true, the `while` loop recycles. If the condition becomes false, the loop is finished.

This concludes your work with the `while` loop. Previously, we pointed out two types of conditions to watch out for when writing `while` loops. The first is to make sure that you create a condition that is true on the first pass, so the loop will perform at least one time. (As you become more adept at C programming, you won't always want your `while` loops performing on a first pass. There will be times when your `while` loops will operate only under certain conditions. But when you start programming in C, you'll find little purpose in designing program code that doesn't work all the time.) The second condition is to make sure that you don't define a condition that can never be false, so that you don't create an endless loop, or a loop you can't break out of short of crashing your program.

Now let's move on to the `do-while` loop. The next section not only expands your knowledge of iteration loops in the C programming language, but it also rounds out a bit more of your knowledge about simple `while` loops.

115

The *do-while* Loop

The `do-while` loop is a variation of the `while` loop. The only difference is the inclusion of the command `do`. But this has a dramatic effect on the `while` loop.

As you learned in the previous section, in a `while` loop the condition is checked first, then the statement or statements are performed depending on the status of the condition. This is called *executing after checking the condition*. The `do-while` loop switches this relationship around and executes the statements before checking the condition. This makes sure that the statements in the loop are always performed at least once.

The basic syntax of the `do-while` loop is as follows:

```
do { statement } while (condition)
```

Because you can use one or more statements in a `do-while` loop, you might find it easier to visualize the basic syntax if it's arranged according to structured code, as follows:

```
do {
    statement1;
    statement2;
    statement3;
```

```
        statement#;
   } while (condition) ;
```

Notice how the condition is placed at the end of the group of statements. The command do enforces the standard sequential processing of commands that follow it. When your computer runs across the do command, it processes the statements that immediately follow the command. When your computer runs into the while (condition), it checks the condition for being true or false.

If the condition is true, your program returns to the do command and runs through the batch of statements that immediately follow it in sequence. These presumably change the condition in some way, which is checked again after all the statements are processed. If the condition remains true, the batch of statements is processed yet again, until the condition becomes false.

When the statement becomes false, your program exits the do loop and proceeds to the next instruction following the loop.

For your first do-while loop, enter the following code for HANG.C. This causes your computer to "hang" in space until you press a key that returns it to the DOS prompt.

```
/* HANG.C */
/* Hangs you computer up until you */
/* press the  A  key */
#include <stdio.h>

main()
{

char stop;

    do {
        scanf("\n%c", &stop);
    }
    while (stop!='a');
}
```

Save this program to disk, then compile and run it.

Type **HANG**.

Press Enter.

Your cursor will move to the left edge of your screen, one line below your DOS prompt, then it will just hang there. You can type other characters if you want to, then press Enter to send them to the program. You'll see these characters appear on the left edge of your screen. None of them, though, will do anything to the program. To quit HANG.EXE, do the following:

Type **a**. *Remember, this means to type a lowercase a, not Shift-A.*

Press Enter.

You should bail out of HANG.EXE and return to your DOS prompt.

This might be a good time to explore the difference between character and integer variables. If you make the following three changes to the code in HANG.C, you can stop the program by entering the number 1.

117

1. Change char stop to int stop.
2. Change \n%c to %d.
3. Change (stop!='a') to (stop!=1).

The following code contains these changes.

```
/* HANG.C */
/* Hangs you computer up until you */
/* press the  1  key */
#include <stdio.h>

main()
{

int stop;

    do {
       scanf("%d",&stop);
    }
    while(stop!=1);
}
```

Save, compile, then run this program.

Type **HANG**.
Press Enter.

As before, your cursor moves to the left edge of your screen below the DOS prompt. To return to your DOS prompt:

Type **1**.
Press Enter.

Watch out! You can enter any number character (0, 1, 2, ..., 9), but you cannot enter a letter character. If you do this, your computer will really hang, and you'll probably have to *cold boot* it (turn it off, then on again). When the `scanf` statement looks for a decimal number ("`%d`"), it expects to find one of those and nothing else. The character variable ("`%c`") is much more forgiving.

break *and* switch

118

The `do` loops are particularly helpful when a choice is involved; for example, the `do-while` loop displays something on-screen that lets you make a choice. Such a thing would most likely be a *menu*.

To see how menus work, you need to understand two additional C programming terms, `break` and `switch`. The `break` keyword breaks you out of a loop. The `switch` keyword takes a variable you've put into the program (from your keyboard) and selects a matching case constant. Regarding menus, the case constant defines what happens when you execute a specific menu command.

Both `switch` and `break` are crucial to menus because a menu presumably contains one of several mutually exclusive choices. This means that you can select only one command on a menu. Once you select the command, you're *switched* to the action attached to the command, and you must *break* out of the loop that draws the menu.

The basic syntax of the `switch` statement is as follows:

```
switch (variable)
   {
   case 1:
     statement;
     break;
```

```
case 2:
   statement;
   break;
case 3:
   statement;
   break;
}
```

The `switch` statement switches you to the appropriate case depending on the value you insert into the variable. For example, typing 1 on your keyboard takes you to `case1`, after which you immediately break out of the loop. Typing 2 takes you to `case2`, and so on.

The trick is to insert the appropriate series of switch case statements in the `do` section of a `do-while` group. If the menu is drawn by the preceding block of `while` statements, then everything works smoothly.

119

Working with more complex `do-while` loops using switch statements might strike you as a bit confusing at first. Take a look at the following code for MENU.C before you enter it.

```
/* MENU.C */
/* Draws a menu on your screen */
/* and lets you select one of three activities */

#include <stdio.h>

main()
{

int select;

    printf("1. Say \"Hello world!\"\n");
    printf("2. Say \"Goodbye world!\".\n");
    printf("3. Continue to think about it.\n");
    printf("Hit any other key to exit.\n");
    printf("    Enter your choice: ");
    do {
      scanf("%d",&select);
      switch(select) {
        case 1:
          printf("Hello world!\n");
          break;
```

```
        case 2:
        printf("Goodbye world!\n");
        break;
        case 3:
        printf("I'm thinking . . .\n");
        break;
        }
    } while (select!=1 && select!=2 && select!=3);
}
```

Once you've written this program, save it to disk, then compile and run the program.

Type **MENU**.

Press Enter.

This runs the first part of your program, which is shown in Figure 8.4.

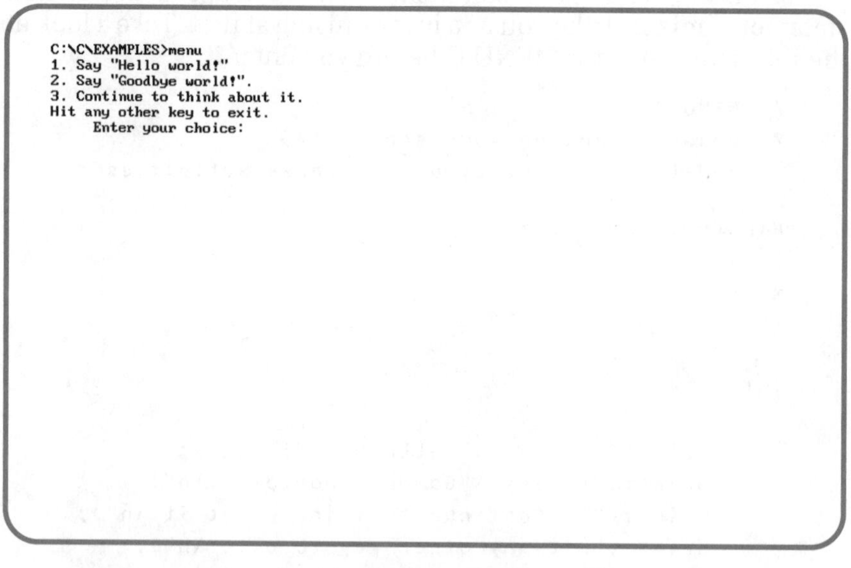

```
C:\C\EXAMPLES>menu
1. Say "Hello world!"
2. Say "Goodbye world!".
3. Continue to think about it.
Hit any other key to exit.
    Enter your choice:
```

Figure 8.4. The displayed menu in MENU.EXE.

To see the rest of the program, press **1**, **2**, or **3**. The appropriate text will be displayed on your screen, and you'll be returned to the DOS prompt, as shown in Figure 8.5.

```
C:\C\EXAMPLES>menu
1. Say "Hello world!"
2. Say "Goodbye world!".
3. Continue to think about it.
Hit any other key to exit.
     Enter your choice: 3
I'm thinking . . .

C:\C\EXAMPLES>
```

Figure 8.5. Results of running MENU.EXE and pressing 3.

121

There are two parts to this program: the section that comes before the do-while loop, and the commands that comprise the do-while loop. The first part displays the menu on your screen. The second part, the do-while loop, performs a command attached to the menu command you select.

Within the do loop there are two parts. The first part consists of two statements: one that scans for your input, the other that matches your input to a specific case. The second part of the do-while loop performs the while statement. The MENU.C program continues to cycle through the three cases until you press the 1, 2, or 3 key. Watch out! If you press any other key, the program will hang, and you'll probably have to cold boot your computer to continue your work.

The do-while condition deserves a bit more explanation. The double ampersand symbol (&&) on the second-to-the-bottom line stands for *logical and*. In this condition, && means that as long as the variable choice does not equal 1, 2 or 3, the condition remains true, so your program will continue to cycle through the cases. Once you press 1, 2, or 3, the condition will become false, and the loop is finished.

The default *Case*

To round out your knowledge about using the switch statement, you should know that you need not use it exclusively with do-while loops. You could write MENU.C without the do-while loop and still make it do the same thing, using the default case. The following code shows how this works.

```
/* MENU.C */
/* Draws a menu on your screen */
/* and lets you select one of three activities */

#include <stdio.h>

main()
{

int select;

        printf("1. Say \"Hello world!\"\n");
        printf("2. Say \"Goodbye world!\".\n");
        printf("3. Continue to think about it.\n");
        printf("Hit any other key to exit.\n");
        printf("      Enter your choice: ");
      scanf("%d",&select);
      switch(select) {
        case 1:
         printf("Hello world!\n");
         break;
        case 2:
         printf("Goodbye world!\n");
         break;
        case 3:
         printf("I'm thinking . . .\n");
         break;
        default:
         printf("No command selected.");
         break;
      }
}
```

Here you have removed the two lines that contain specific instructions for the do-while loop: the line containing do { and the line containing } while (select!=1 && select!=2 && select!=3);.

If you save, compile, and run MENU.EXE now, you'll be given the same menu you saw earlier. The only difference is that now, if you press any key other than 1, 2, or 3, which are assigned to switch cases, the program defaults to the default case, which tells you that you didn't select a command. The loop is broken, and you're returned to the DOS prompt.

Summary

In this chapter, you completed your preliminary knowledge of iterative loops. To do this, you learned how to work with `while` and `do-while` loops.

The only difference between a `while` loop and a `do-while` loop is that the `while` loop checks the condition first before it performs the statement. A `do-while` loop performs the statement first, then checks the condition.

In the next chapter, you'll learn about arrays and how you use them with strings and numbers.

123

Chapter 9

Arrays, Strings, and Numbers

In This Chapter

In this chapter, you'll learn about how you create arrays and use them to manipulate strings and numbers. This work will expand your ability to handle different data types. It will also help you handle larger and more complex sections of text, as well as lists—or databases—of numbers.

What Is an Array?

An array is a programming concept that defines how data is maintained in a program. Almost all computer programs are designed to handle data in some manner. For example, in this book we've written programs that convert Fahrenheit to centigrade, display the ASCII character set, and count numbers on your screen. These temperatures, characters, and numbers are all forms of data. So far, we have been focusing on how to write instructions for extracting or manipulating data. But, of course, our overall concern—the purpose of our programs—involves the nature of the data and the way it's displayed.

The best way to understand the concept of arrays is to visualize an array as a database, or a base of data that you want to maintain and manipulate. The data can be in the form of characters or numbers, such as the names and addresses of people and their telephone numbers that you want to maintain in your personal electronic phone book.

Arrays support all four data types: characters, integers, float, and double. There is a fifth data type called *void* which is used for high level work. We won't use that type in this book.

Before you can use an array, you must first define its structure using a statement. This lets your C compiler know how much space it must reserve for the array and its data contents.

To define the structure of an array, use the following basic format:

```
type [name] [size]
```

First, specify the data type you want to use, such as character (`char`) or integer (`int`). Next, give the array a name. You can use any string of characters that doesn't conflict with those in the C glossary, such as keywords or variable names (for example, you can't use `break` or `char`). Finally, specify the size of the array—how many elements will be contained in the array.

As an example, say that you want to create an array that holds 26 alphabet characters. To create the array called *alpha*, use the following statement:

```
char alpha[26]
```

This example creates 26 character variables with names ranging from `alpha[0]` to `alpha[25]`. The first element of an array is always given the number 0. This means that the number of the last element will always be one less than the total number of elements (26−1=25).

126

Multi-Dimensional Arrays

You can create *multi-dimensional* arrays by using multiple numbers of arrays. Just declare the dimension after the size using the following basic syntax:

```
type name [size1] [size2]
```

The following example creates a two-dimensional array called `name` with 100 items containing characters:

```
char name[50][2]
```

In this case, the numbering system is a bit different than it is for single-dimension arrays (which is the type you first learned about in this chapter). The 100 elements of a multi-dimensional array are assigned numbers in pairs. For example, in the two-dimensional array `char name[50][2]`, the elements are numbered in the following sequence:

```
name[0][0]
name[0][1]
name[1][0]
name[1][1]
name[2][0]
name[2][1]
name[3][0]
  .  .  .  .
name[49][1]
```

127

The numbering scheme remains the same; that is, each sequence begins with 0 and ends with one less than the number of the size or dimension.

The following example creates a three-dimensional array called `name` with 1,000 elements:

```
char name[50][2][10]
```

Creating an array is no more difficult than inserting such a statement in the proper place in one of your programs. The trick comes when you begin inserting data into elements of the array. You can insert all sorts of data into an array, with the two broad types being characters and numbers.

Planning Beforehand

When you design an array, you need to have a clear idea in mind of the sort of information you want to store in the array, as well as the size and extent of the information.

The biggest problem to watch out for when working with arrays is that you don't insert more data into an array than can fit. Some programs, such as database and spreadsheet programs, prevent you from entering excess information, but this is not true of the C programming language. If you create an array and then try to squeeze in more data than will fit, the data may very well be stored elsewhere in your program, overwriting values in other variables. This will cause your program to perform incorrectly, at the very least, and most likely will cause your program to crash and not run at all.

You'll learn how to plan ahead for the size and extent of your data as you begin to work with examples in this chapter. Even though we've worked with numbers extensively in this book, we'll start working with arrays using strings, because they are most suitable for single-dimension arrays. Later in the book, we'll switch to numbers in arrays, and use multi-dimensional arrays.

Working with Strings

Broadly speaking, a string is any series of characters strung together to form a single element, such as this sentence you're reading now. The element is the sentence.

In C programming, a string is any series of characters terminated by the null character 0. This null character is not the character 0 (zero), which is ASCII character decimal 48. (ASCII decimal 49 is 1, 50 is 2, and so on.) The null character is ASCII decimal 0, or hex 00, which comes at the very beginning of the ASCII character set and has no symbol at all. Its three-letter code is NUL. In C programming, when you want to insert a null character after a string, you use the backslash code \0 (see Table 9.1).

Table 9.1. Table codes and their meanings.

Code	Meaning
\a	Alert
\b	Backspace
\f	Form feed
\n	New line
\r	Carriage return
\t	Horizontal tab
\v	Vertical tab
\x#	Hexadecimal constant (#=hex number)
\#	Octal constant (#=octal number)
\0	Null
\\	Backslash
\'	Single quote character
\"	Double quote character

When you declare an array that will hold a string, you must create enough space to hold all the characters. You must also add one more space to hold the null terminator. For example, to create an array called `city` that will hold strings of up to 15 characters, you would use the following syntax:

```
char city[16]
```

The array type for strings is character (`char`), the array name is `city`, and the array size is 16, which can hold up to 15 string characters.

For your first example of working with a string array, type the following code for CITY.C. This lets you put a city name into an array, then displays the string contents on your screen.

```
/* CITY.C */
/* Simple string array */
#include <stdio.h>

main()
{
char city[16];
```

```
printf("Type a city name, then press [Enter].");
    printf("\n");
    gets(city);

    printf("This is your string: %s",city);
}
```

There's one new instruction in this program: `gets`. This stands for *get string*, and will get or retrieve the string assigned to the array `city`.

Save this file to disk, then compile and run the program.

Type **CITY**.
Press Enter.

The first part of the program asks you to enter a city name.

Type **CROTON**.
Press Enter.

130

The program will display your string and return you to your DOS prompt, as shown in Figure 9.1.

```
C:\C\EXAMPLES>city
Type a city name, then press [Enter].
CROTON
This is your string: CROTON
C:\C\EXAMPLES>
```

Figure 9.1. Results of running CITY.EXE.

There's nothing spectacular in CITY.EXE. In fact, it's not as complicated as the second program you wrote in this book, which converted your age in years to the equivalent in months.

The purpose of writing CITY.C is to get a feel for the way strings are handled, and to see what happens when you stuff too many characters into an array.

Try running CITY.EXE a second time, but put in a much longer city name.

Type **CITY**.

Press Enter.

Type **CROTON-ON-THE-HUDSON**.

Press Enter.

As before, the city name will be displayed as the string, but you'll also get a DOS error message or your computer will lock up (depending upon the compiler you use). You've stuffed too many characters into your array.

131

Common String Library Functions

The best way to understand more about strings and arrays is to learn how to use the more common C library string functions. The following two string functions are the most interesting and will be described in more detail in this section:

`strcat()`   Stands for *string concatenation*. Adds the contents of one string to another string.

`strcmp()`   Stands for *string compare*. Compares two strings and returns a zero if they are identical.

These two new functions are located in the header file called STRING.H, which contains all sorts of string library functions. Figure 9.2 shows the top of the contents of this file.

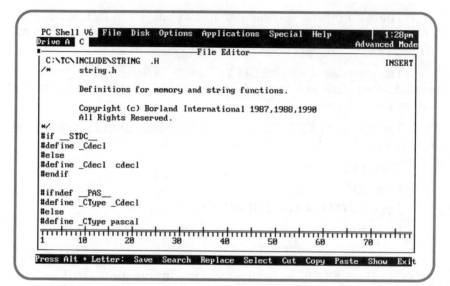

Figure 9.2. Top of the contents of STRING.H.

The exact contents of the file STRING.H that you look at might vary from that shown in Figure 9.2, depending upon which compiler you're using.

You'll have to include this header file name STRING.H at the top of any program which tries to access a string function. You include STRING.H as follows: `#include "string.h"`.

strcat

The `strcat()` function combines—or concatenates—the contents of two separate strings into one string, the first string. The second string is left unchanged.

The basic format for the `strcat()` function is as follows:

```
strcat(string1, string2)
```

To use the `strcat()` function correctly, you have to load characters into each string, then combine the strings.

For example, the following program combines a common C language greeting with your name (which you can substitute for my name).

```
/* COMBINE.C */
/* Combines or concatenates two strings */
#include <stdio.h>
#include <string.h>

main()
{

char fname[40], lname[20];

    printf("Type your first name for the first string.\n");
    printf("Then press [Spacebar] and [Enter].\n");
    gets(fname);

    printf("Type your last name for the second string.");
    printf("Then press [Enter] again.\n");
    gets(lname);

    strcat(fname,lname);
    printf("Your name is %s",fname);
}
```

133

This program contains the new header file "string.h" at the top of the program. It also defines the two string arrays economically, on the same line. As long as both arrays are of an identical type, you can define them on the same line.

But take a closer look at the sizes of the two arrays. The array `fname` stands for first name, and the array `lname` stands for last name. But why is the first array twice as big as the second? Because it will have to contain all the characters in both the first and second arrays when they are combined, or concatenated. Remember, if you overload an array with too many characters, you run the risk of crashing your program. You must define arrays with enough room to hold all the characters you want.

Now save COMBINE.C, then compile and run it.

Type **COMBINE**.
Press Enter.

When you're asked your first name, type it in. Be sure to press the spacebar before you press Enter so that you can separate your first and last names with an empty space. Next, type your last name, then press Enter. Your complete name should be displayed on your screen, as mine is in Figure 9.3.

```
C:\C\EXAMPLES>combine
Type your first name for the first string.
Then press [Spacebar] and [Enter].
Charles
Type your last name for the second string.Then press [Enter] again.
Ackerman
Your name is Charles Ackerman
C:\C\EXAMPLES>
```

134

Figure 9.3. Results of running COMBINE.EXE.

Look back at the code for COMBINE.C. Notice that the contents of the two arrays fname and lname, which you filled with your first and last name, respectively, are combined on the second-to-last line of the program and placed in the first array fname, which is then displayed.

strcmp

The strcmp() function compares the contents of two string arrays and returns the value of 0 if the two are equal. If the first string is larger than the second, strcmp() returns the difference between the two as a positive value. If the first string is smaller than the second, the function returns the difference between the two as a negative value.

The basic format for the strcmp() function is as follows:

```
strcmp(string1, string2)
```

To use the strcmp() function correctly, you must load characters into each string, then combine the strings.

A common use for strcmp() is in a password routine. This checks user input against a recorded password. If the user enters the correct password, the program can continue. If the user doesn't enter the correct password, he can be given a second chance or the program can exit.

The following program shows you a password example that lets the user try again.

```c
/* PASSWORD.C */
/* Checks a user's password against */
/* one stored in the program */
#include <stdio.h>
#include <string.h>

main()
{

char password20;
int num;
    do {
      printf("Enter your password :");
      gets(password);
    }
    while(strcmp(password,"open sesame"));

    printf("1. Say \"Hello world!\"\n");
    printf("2. Say \"Goodbye world!\".\n");
    printf("3. Continue to think about it.\n");
    printf("Hit any other key to exit.\n");
    printf("     Enter your choice: ");
    do {
      scanf("%d",&num);
      switch(num) {
        case 1:
          printf("Hello world!\n");
          break;
        case 2:
          printf("Goodbye world!\n");
          break;
        case 3:
          printf("I'm thinking . . .\n");
          break;
        }
    } while (num!=1 && num!=2 && num!=3);
}
```

We'll describe the details of this program as soon as you run it. For the moment, just be aware that the secret password is *open sesame* (you might want to use another password if you ever include this code in your own programs).

Save PASSWORD.C, then compile and run it.

Type **PASSWORD**.
Press Enter.

The first part of the program, the part that checks for your password, asks for your password.

Type **MOM**.
Press Enter.

You're asked again for the password. This time, type anything you want and press Enter. As long as you don't enter *open sesame*, you'll continue to cycle through the `do-while` loop that requests your password.

OK, let's proceed with the program.

Type **open sesame**.
Press Enter.

Now the program proceeds. Select a number to end the program.

Let's take a closer look at the password part of the program. A character type array called `password` is defined for 20 characters. You can find the password itself further down in the `do-while` loop, in the second string for the `strcmp()` function. Remember, the syntax for `strcmp()` is `strcmp(string1, string2)`, in which `string2` is compared to `string1`. In PASSWORD.C, the function appears as follows: `strcmp(password,"open sesame")`. `String2` is the password `open sesame`. `String1` is the `password` array, which you fill with whatever you type from your keyboard.

As soon as you press Enter, the program checks your input against the stored value `open sesame`. There's an interesting twist here, however, and that's because a `do-while` continues only as long as the `while` condition is true. You'd think that an exact match between `string1` and `string2` would yield true, but that's not the case. When `string1` and `string2` match in the `strcmp()` function, a value of 0 is returned. This number is assigned to false. Any other value is considered true.

This means that when you finally enter `open sesame`, `strcmp()` analyzes the match, finds it perfect, returns 0 to your computer, which is determined to be false. The condition no longer being true, the loop is broken, and you proceed to the next part of the program.

You might recognize the last part of PASSWORD.C as MENU.C, which you wrote in the previous chapter. You could include any of the programs you've written so far in this section, or any other program that works. The point of this example is to show you how the password routine permits or forbids you to continue with any program.

There are other string functions in STRING.H you might want to become familiar with. The best way to do this is locate their definitions in Appendix B and experiment with them in short programs.

The rest of this chapter is devoted to working with numbers in arrays.

137

Working with Numbers

Working with numbers in arrays is not much different from working with strings. In fact, some numbers are no different from strings at all. This is particularly true of single numbers, such as phone numbers and ZIP codes. Numerical codes such as these have no value other than what they signify: a number to call or an address.

Numbers become important in arrays only when you want to store large quantities of them and refer to them periodically, and use them in calculations from time to time. Some examples are finding the total of many receipts for a single day, calculating the average temperature over a year, or adjusting the current balance in a checking account.

When you want to load a series of individual numbers into an array in your computer's memory, you'll have to modify the basic syntax of the array definition, as follows:

```
type name [size1] [size2] [size..] = { list };
```

The change appears as the last part of this syntax. The numbers you want to load into the array will appear within a bracketed list followed by a semicolon.

As an example, let's create a two-dimensional array that displays the square value of a decimal number you put into the program. To create this program, type the following code for SQUARE.C

```
/* CONVERT.C */
/* Displays the cubed value of a number between 1 and 10 */
#include <stdio.h>

int cube[10][2] = {
     1, 1,
     2, 8,
     3, 27,
     4, 64,
     5, 125,
     6, 216,
     7, 343,
     8, 512,
     9, 729,
     10, 1000,};

main()
{

int a, b;

printf ("Enter a number between 0 and 10: \n");
     scanf("%d", &a);

     for(b=0; b<10; b++)
       if(cubeb0==a) break;
     printf("The cube of \"%d\" is %d\n", a, cubeb1);
}
```

Now save the file, then compile and run it.

Type **CONVERT**.

Press Enter.

You're first asked to enter a value.

Type **5**.

Press Enter.

The program should reply that the cube of 5 is 125, as shown in Figure 9.4.

```
C:\C\EXAMPLES>convert
5
The cube of "5" is 125

C:\C\EXAMPLES>
```

139

Figure 9.4. Results of running CONVERT.EXE.

You can try some other numbers if you want to guarantee that this program works correctly.

Understanding CONVERT.C

You should take a closer look at the contents of CONVERT.C so that you can understand how numbers work with arrays.

The first part of CONVERT.C creates the two-dimensional array and contains the bracketed list of values we want to insert into the array. These are the 10 decimal numbers 1 to 10 matched with their cubed values ($1^3=1$, $2^3=8$, $3^3=27$, and so on).

It might be easier for you to visualize the numbers being stored in the array as if they were being placed into bins in your computer's memory, bins that look something like the following:

	0	1
1	1	1
2	2	8
3	3	27
4	4	64
5	5	125
6	6	216
7	7	343
8	8	512
9	9	729
10	10	1000

140

The vertical row of numbers down the left side of this visual array corresponds to the first dimension size of the array, whereas the horizontal row of numbers across the top of the array corresponds to the second dimension size of the array. The individual number pairs have been inserted in each bin. For example, 3 occupies bin 3,0, whereas its cube value of 27 occupies the bin 3,1.

The second part of CONVERT.C code begins by asking you to enter a number between 1 and 10. After you respond by giving the program a number, the program proceeds to look for the number in the first column of the array (a). If it finds the number, the program then locates its matching value in the second column (b) and displays it.

You can change the number pairs to square values, or any other equivalency. All the program needs are two rows of numbers, with the first column containing possible input and the second column containing possible output.

There are other things you can do with numbers as well. You can store calculated values based upon numbers you put into the program, such as tax charges. But this sort of programming requires that you know more about inserting functions and making calls to these functions.

Summary

In this chapter, you learned how to work with arrays, strings, and numbers. Arrays are perhaps the trickiest feature of the three. You'll find strings handy for working with longer sections of text. And you'll find numbers handy for working with all sorts of figures.

Now that you've learned more about numbers, you might want to find out various ways that numbers can be handled in programming. The next chapter describes programming notational systems, and how they can help your learning how to program in C.

141

Numbering Systems and Display Formats

In This Chapter

In Chapter 4, you learned how to display some characters in the ASCII character set. In Chapter 5, you learned more about the ASCII character set.

In this chapter, you'll be introduced to the three most popular number schemes, or notational systems, used in programming. The three systems are decimal, hexadecimal, and binary. We presume you already know something about the decimal system, although we'll define this system as a way of introducing the others.

Along the way, you'll learn how to display number values using the various types of notational systems, as well as how to change the appearance or format of displayed numbers, which can apply to all characters.

You can avoid learning anything about number systems and still become a C programmer. But you won't become an adept programmer without some knowledge of the popular types of numbering systems. And you'll never understand the fundamental operation of computers and programming languages.

What Are Number Systems?

Number systems are used to represent values. For example, in the English measurement system, 12 inches make a foot and three feet make a yard. These are number values that represent distance. There are other number values that represent distance as well. In the metric measurement system, 100 centimeters make a meter (which is a little longer than a yard) and 1,000 meters make a kilometer. In the American distance system, 5,280 feet—or 1,760 yards—make one mile, which is about half again as long as a kilometer.

Although all this might sound confusing (it does to me), all you need to know is that when you take 10 steps, you're going to cover a certain distance no matter how you measure it. How you measure it—and the numbers you give the units—depends upon what system you want to use.

The number system we're most familiar with is called the decimal system. The name comes from the Latin root *decem*, which means ten. There's no secret to how we came to use a system based on the number 10. Because we have ten fingers, it's easiest to count in groups of 10.

There are other number systems we can use. They're just harder to visualize because they use a different base number. In fact, each system gets its name from its unique base number.

Binary	Uses base 2 displayed in the two digits 0 and 1 only.
Octal	Uses base 8 displayed in groups of eight consecutive decimal digits.
Decimal	Uses base 10 displayed in the ten digits 0, 1, 2, 3, 4, 5, 6, 7, 8 and 9.
Hexadecimal	Uses base 16 displayed in the 10 digits 0, 1, 2, 3, 4, 5, 6, 7, 8, 9, A, B, C, D, E and F.

You can get a better idea of the relationships among these four notational systems if you compare some decimal values you're familiar with to their equivalents in the other three systems, as shown in Table 10.1.

Table 10.1. Values in the four most popular notational systems.

Decimal	Octal	Binary	Hexadecimal
0	0	0000	0
1	1	0001	1
2	2	0010	2
3	3	0011	3
4	4	0100	4
5	5	0101	5
6	6	0110	6
7	7	0111	7
8	10	1000	8
9	11	1001	9
10	12	1010	A
11	13	1011	B
12	14	1100	C
13	15	1101	D
14	16	1110	E
15	17	1111	F
16	20	10000	10
17	21	10001	11
18	22	10010	12
19	23	10011	13
20	24	10100	14
..	..	..	..
100	144	1100100	64

145

For most of our daily activities, the decimal system is perfectly acceptable. We run into a problem only when we try to use decimal numbers for programming. Because the number 2 is not a root factor of 10, it's difficult to translate decimal numbers into the binary system. The binary system is important because it's the fundamental system used by your computer. You'll find out how this works in the next section. Then you'll expand upon this knowledge to see why the hexadecimal system is superior for programming notation.

The Binary Notational System

The binary notational system is based on the number 2. In this system, numbers are represented by sequences of 1s and 0s. For example, the number one looks like this: 0001. The number two looks like this: 0010. And the number 10 looks like this: 1010. You can find more equivalents in Table 10.1.

The binary system gets its name from the fact that *binary* means *made up of two parts or things*. The importance of the binary system can be seen when you understand how your computer stores data. The heart of your computer, the CPU, as well as every memory chip, is for the most part a series of transistors. A transistor is an electrical switch, and can exist in either an *on* or an *off* state.

The state depends upon whether the transistor is charged or not. When a transistor is charged, it's on. Symbolically, this state is given the number 1. When a transistor is off, it is not charged. Symbolically, this state is given the number 0.

All data, including that stored in your computer's memory as well as data stored on disk, is maintained in your computer's memory as a series of 1s and 0s. This means that a long series of transistors in your computer, when holding data, looks something like this symbolically: 1101010001100. This data includes everything, from the program files that run your word processor and communications program, to the spreadsheets, database files, and text documents you work with.

Whenever you compile a program, such as when you compile the C programs you've designed in this book, you convert the characters to binary format. Every instruction you insert into a program, from `main()` to `printf("I love you");`, is converted to binary format on disk. Because everything is eventually processed in your computer as on and off bits, the binary system is the most fundamental you can use.

Working with the Binary System

You can convert a binary number to decimal format by entering the values of each binary digit into a formula. Let's use as an example the binary number 1010. You can see from the table that the decimal equivalent is 10, but let's find out how this occurs through conversion. Begin with the rightmost digit and multiply it by the number 2 taken to the power of its position. The first digit is always in position 0 and the second digit is in position 1. Always work from the right side towards the left through the binary digits, calculating the value of each digit, and then sum the values according to the following formula:

$$(1 \times 2^3) + (0 \times 2^2) + (1 \times 2^1) + (0 \times 2^0)$$

Notice how the rightmost digit, 0, is multiplied by 2 raised to the power of 0, which means that the digit is in the first position. The second digit from the right, 1, is multiplied by 2 raised to the power of 1, which means that the digit is in the second position. The third digit, 0, is multiplied by 2 raised to the power of 2, which means that the digit is in the third position, and so on. The following steps show how to calculate the total:

1. The first parenthetical group on the right yields the number 0, because any number multiplied by 0 results in 0. You don't have to bother calculating the value of 0 binary digits. Zeros are used only to fill out the proper order of digits.

2. The second parenthetical group from the right yields the number 2, because 2^1 results in 2, and $1 \times 2 = 2$.

3. The third parenthetical group from the right, like the first, yields the number 0.

4. The fourth parenthetical group from the right yields the number 8, because 2^3 is 8, and $8 \times 1 = 8$.

147

You get a total of 10 when you add the results of each group this way: $8 + 0 + 2 + 0$.

The following is a more graphic depiction of these calculations:

Binary symbol: 1010
Equation: $(1 \times 2^3) + (0 \times 2^2) + (1 \times 2^1) + (0 \times 2^0)$
Results: $8 + 0 + 2 + 0 = 10$

All this calculating goes on automatically and very quickly when your computer places into memory the data you put on your screen. Similarly, a quick translation occurs when your computer reads data from memory or a disk and places it on your screen. Computer data is stored in both your computer's memory and on disk in binary form, because this is the only way minute levels of electricity can work reliably. (Like old fashioned lights, a binary digit is either on or off. There are no rheostats for computer memory that vary the amount of electricity being used).

Problems Working with the Binary System

There are two problems you'll run across when working with values in the binary system. The first is that they are tedious to write down. Four digits are usually included at the minimum, so the decimal number 1 is shown as 0001. This means you have to write four digits for one small value.

Second, when the size of your values begins to rise, the length of the binary equivalent expands even faster. For example, the decimal 100 is equal to the binary 1100100. That's seven digits.

The decimal system isn't much better to use. True, it takes fewer digits than the binary system, but the number 2 is not a root factor of 10. Ten can be divided by 2, but that doesn't make 2 a root factor. Powers are squares, cubes, and other values that result when you multiply a number by itself. For example, 2 x 2 = 4, so 4 is a power of 2. Four is the square of 2, which is usually shown as 2^2. And 2 x 2 x 2 = 8, which makes 8 a power of two—the cube of 2—usually shown as 2^3. Each notational system is identified by the base it uses: 2 for binary, 8 for octal, 10 for decimal and 16 for hexadecimal. Only three of these have 2 as a root factor: the decimal system does not.

Let's take a look at a comparison of identical values for all four notational systems. Here are the matching values for decimal 100, as shown in Table 10.1.

Decimal	Octal	Binary	Hexadecimal
100	144	1100100	64

Notice that the binary value requires seven digits (1100100), the octal and decimal values require three digits (although the decimal just barely), whereas the hexadecimal system requires only two digits. The higher the base used by a notational system, the fewer digits it takes to represent a value.

The next power after cube is quadruple. When you quadruple the value of 2, you get 16 (2 x 2 x 2 x 2). This is displayed as 2^4. The number 16 is the base of the hexadecimal system, which is the most appropriate one to use with today's computer technology to display values. You'll find out why in the next section.

The Hexadecimal System

You can actually gain some practical value when you learn about the hexadecimal system, because the Norton Utilities lets you view the contents of both data and program files in hexadecimal format and change these contents if you want to. Naturally, you have to know what you're doing before you make any changes, and understanding the hexadecimal system is the first step towards making these changes successfully.

The hexadecimal—or *hex*—system operates on a base of 16. As pointed out, the hex system, when compared to the binary, octal, and decimal systems, requires the fewest number of digits to represent a value. For a hex value to require three digits, you need to go past decimal 1000.

The value of working with fewer digits is that it takes less time to write them down. When you get into number intensive calculations, this efficiency can become a real advantage.

149

Let's take a closer look at the anatomy of hex numbering. Whereas the binary system has 2 numbers (0 and 1) and the decimal system has 10 numbers (0 to 9), the hex system with base 16 must have 16 numbers. And it does—0 to F. That's right: 0, 1, 2, 3, 4, 5, 6, 7, 8, 9, A, B, C, D, E and F. The letter A corresponds to the decimal number 10, and the letter F corresponds to the decimal number 15. Because the ten integers 0 through 9 were originally created with the decimal system in mind, the designers of the hex system needed six new symbols for their system. They chose the first six letters of the alphabet because they wanted to use symbols with which everyone was already familiar.

Actually, the preferred method for writing hex numbers is to use a two-digit symbol, so 0 is shown as 00, 1 is 01, 2 is 02, 10 is 0A, and 15 is 0F. It's perfectly acceptable to mix numbers with letters like that, because in the hex system the letters are numbers.

To complete your understanding of how hex numbers work, we'll take a look at a few more examples using decimal equivalents.

The hex equivalent of the decimal number 16 is 10. Why 10? Well, in the decimal system, it's the beginning of the second set of numbers (10, 11, 12, and on to 19).

In the hexadecimal system, 10 also begins the second set of digits, but its equivalent decimal value is 16. Hex 11 is decimal 17, hex 12 is decimal 18, and so on to hex 19, which is decimal 25. This is where things take a strange hex twist. Decimal 26 is 1A. Why is that? Well, A is the next hex number past 9. This means that the first hex number past hex 19 would have to be 1A. Decimal 27 is 1B, decimal 28 is 1C, and so on up to decimal 32, which is hex 20. This is where the third set of hex numbers begins.

If this is your first introduction to the hex system, by now you either have the idea down pat, or you don't. Therefore, either you're ready to move on to something new, or you're ready to take a break with plans of returning to this section later for further clarification.

In the next section, you'll learn how to design several programs that display numbers in different notational systems. This will help you teach yourself about the equivalence of values across all notational systems. It will also teach you how to work more precisely with several format codes, and how to format your screen displays.

Displaying Numbers in Various Systems

In the previous section, you learned about various notational systems. You should already be familiar with the decimal system. You should realize that the binary notational system is fundamental to computers. And you should realize that much of programming with numbers is done using the hexadecimal system.

With the following program, you'll be able to enter a decimal value which will be converted to its hexadecimal equivalent.

```
/* HEXCONV.C */
/* Converts decimal input to hexadecimal equivalent */
#include <stdio.h>

main()
{
int number;
```

```
printf("Type a decimal value, then press [Enter : \n");
scanf("%d", &number);
printf("Its hex equivalent is %x", number);
}
```

Save this program, then compile and run it.

Type **HEXCONV**.
Press Enter.

The program asks you to type a decimal number, then press Enter.

Type **16**.
Press Enter.

The program replies with 10, as shown in Figure 10.1.

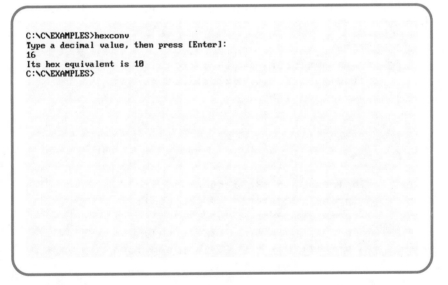

```
C:\C\EXAMPLES>hexconv
Type a decimal value, then press [Enter]:
16
Its hex equivalent is 10
C:\C\EXAMPLES>
```

Figure 10.1. Results of running HEXCONV.EXE.

You should try a couple of other decimal numbers as well. Just press F3, type a new decimal number, then press Enter. If you try decimal numbers lower than 10, you'll find their hex equivalents identical.

The program HEXCONV.C is fairly simple. You declare an integer variable called num that stores the figure you put in from the keyboard. Initially, the number is taken in as a decimal value using `scanf("%d", &num)`. The next line converts the number to its hex equivalent using the format specified in `%x`. Refer to Table 4.3 for a list of the format codes you can use.

There are two format codes that let you display hexadecimal values: `%x` and `%X`. The first displays hex numbers using lowercase letters; the second displays uppercase letters. Because you'll view most hex numbers in uppercase format, you might want to change the way hex numbers are displayed using HEXCONV.EXE. Just change the `%x` to `%X` in the last line of the program, as follows: `printf("Its hex equivalent is %X", num);`.

If you take a closer look at the format codes in Table 4.3, you'll see that you can use four different codes to display numbers in various types of notational systems: `%d` for decimal, `%o` for octal, `%x` for hexadecimal lowercase, and `%X` for hexadecimal uppercase.

You can write the following program to display the series of decimal numbers from 1 to 20 using all four types of notational display.

```
/* NOTATE.C */
/* Displays numbers in three notational formats */
/* including the two hexadecimal formats */
#include <stdio.h>

main()
{
int num;

    for(num=0; num<20; num++) {
       printf("decimal    %d ", num);
       printf("octal    %o ", num);
       printf("hex lc    %x ", num);
       printf("hex uc    %X\n", num);
   }
}
```

In this program, `lc` stands for lowercase and `uc` stands for uppercase.

Save this program, then compile and run it.

Type **NOTATE**.

Press Enter.

A stream of characters in four columns will flow upwards on your screen, to end with the display shown in Figure 10.2.

```
C:\C\EXAMPLES>notate
decimal    0 octal    0 hex lc    0 hex uc    0
decimal    1 octal    1 hex lc    1 hex uc    1
decimal    2 octal    2 hex lc    2 hex uc    2
decimal    3 octal    3 hex lc    3 hex uc    3
decimal    4 octal    4 hex lc    4 hex uc    4
decimal    5 octal    5 hex lc    5 hex uc    5
decimal    6 octal    6 hex lc    6 hex uc    6
decimal    7 octal    7 hex lc    7 hex uc    7
decimal    8 octal   10 hex lc    8 hex uc    8
decimal    9 octal   11 hex lc    9 hex uc    9
decimal   10 octal   12 hex lc    a hex uc    A
decimal   11 octal   13 hex lc    b hex uc    B
decimal   12 octal   14 hex lc    c hex uc    C
decimal   13 octal   15 hex lc    d hex uc    D
decimal   14 octal   16 hex lc    e hex uc    E
decimal   15 octal   17 hex lc    f hex uc    F
decimal   16 octal   20 hex lc   10 hex uc   10
decimal   17 octal   21 hex lc   11 hex uc   11
decimal   18 octal   22 hex lc   12 hex uc   12
decimal   19 octal   23 hex lc   13 hex uc   13

C:\C\EXAMPLES>
```

Figure 10.2. Results of running NOTATE.EXE.

You should recognize the component parts of NOTATE.C. First, you define an integer variable as `number`. The `for loop` that follows prepares the program to cycle through the first 20 numbers. The four `printf` statements print the 20 numbers in four different formats.

Formatted Display

Once you start printing columns of numbers, you might want to arrange the columns so that they appear in a better format on your screen. To adjust the format of characters printed on your screen, you will use *formatting specifiers*, of which there are three: minimum field width specifier, precision specifier, and justifying specifier.

Minimum Field Width Specifier

The minimum field width specifier, when added to a `printf` state-ment, can extend a number with a specified minimum width, or number of spaces. The best way to see how this works is to type the code for WIDTH.C, then run the program.

```
/* WIDTH.C */
/* Demonstrates field width specifier */
#include <stdio.h>

main()
{

int example;
example = 10;

printf("The example is: %d\n", example);
printf("Example padded width twenty spaces: %20d\n", example);
printf("Example padded with twenty 0s: %020d\n", example);
}
```

Now save the file, then compile and run it.

Type **WIDTH**.

Press Enter.

Your screen should look something like Figure 10.3.

You are given a display of the sample number, then the same number padded to 20 spaces with blanks, then the number padded again to 20 spaces with zeros.

If you refer back to the code for WIDTH.C, you'll notice that you start out declaring an integer called `example`, then you specify the value of the variable to be 10. Next you insert three `printf` statements. The first displays the example, the second displays the example with 18 blank spaces preceding the example number, and the third displays the example with 18 zeros preceding the number.

When you wrote the second and third `printf` statements, you were instructing your C compiler to create number displays, each with a total of 20 spaces. Only two of these digits are taken up by the number 10 itself. The remainder are padded out, on the first line with blank spaces, on the second line with leading zeros.

```
C:\C\EXAMPLES>width
The example is: 10
Example padded width twenty spaces:                    10
Example padded with twenty 0s: 000000000000000000010

C:\C\EXAMPLES>
```

Figure 10.3. Results of running WIDTH.EXE.

155

If you use minimum width specifiers at all, you'll most likely employ them to format the display of items on your screen. For example, you can use them to create columns of items running down your screen, or to separate individual items by a certain number of spaces on a single line of your screen.

Precision Specifier

The precision specifier lets you specify the appearance of data for integers, strings, and floating point numbers. The basic syntax is as follows:

```
%[mws] .[ps] [data]
```

The term mws stands for *minimum width specifier*, whereas ps stands for *precision specifier*.

When used with integers, the precision specifier controls how many digits will appear in each number. For example, %5.10d will display an integer with a minimum of five numbers 10 digits long. If the number is less than 10 digits, zeros will be added before the number so that the number totals 10 digits.

When used with strings, the precision specifier controls the maximum length of the string. For example, the precision specifier %.5s will display a string of characters a minimum of five spaces long and a maximum of 10 spaces. If the string is shorter than five spaces, blank spaces will be added. If the string is longer than 10 spaces, the characters extending beyond that limit will not be displayed.

When used with floating point numbers, the precision specifier controls how many decimal point digits will appear. For example, %.5f will display a number with five decimal point numbers regardless of how many decimal numbers exist.

You can use a minimum width specifier along with a precision specifier, but you don't have to. The following code gives you an example of how each example of a precision specifier works.

```
/* PRECISE.C */
/* Demonstrates the precision specifier */
#include <stdio.h>

main()
{
    printf("12345 printed as: %5.10d\n", 12345);
    printf("ABCDEFGHI printed as: %.5s\n", "ABCDEFGH");
    printf("1.1234567 printed as: %.5f\n", 1.1234567);
}
```

Save this file, then compile and run it.

Type **PRECISE**.

Press Enter.

Your screen should look something like Figure 10.4.

After running this program, you might want to change some of the precision specifiers and number values, and see what effect the changes have.

Justified Output

You can alter the position where displayed fields appear on your screen by using the minus sign (–) just after the percentage symbol for left justified display. Otherwise, fields normally appear justified on the right.

```
C:\C\EXAMPLES>precise
12345 printed as: 0000012345
ABCDEFGHI printed as: ABCDE
1.1234567 printed as: 1.12346

C:\C\EXAMPLES>
```

Figure 10.4. Results of running PRECISE.EXE.

157

The following program contains sample code you can use to experiment with minus right and left justified output.

```c
/* LEFTJUST.C */
/* Demonstrates the precision specifier */
#include <stdio.h>

main()
{
    printf("ABCDEFGHI right justified as: %10s\n", "ABCDEFGH");
    printf("ABCDEFGHI left justified as: %-10s\n", "ABCDEFGH");
    printf("12345 right justified as: %10d\n", 12345);
    printf("12345 left justified as: %-10d\n", 12345);
    printf("1.1234567 right justified as: %10f\n", 1.1234567);
    printf("1.1234567 left justified as: %-10f\n", 1.1234567);
}
```

Save this file, then compile and run it.

Type **LEFTJUST**.
Press Enter.

Your screen should change to look something like Figure 10.5.

```
C:\C\EXAMPLES>leftjust
ABCDEFGHI right justified as:    ABCDEFGH
ABCDEFGHI left justified as: ABCDEFGH
12345 right justified as:       12345
12345 left justified as: 12345
1.1234567 right justified as:   1.123457
1.1234567 left justified as: 1.123457

C:\C\EXAMPLES>
```

Figure 10.5. Results of running LEFTJUST.EXE.

Summary

In this chapter, you learned more about the various notational systems you can use to display and calculate numbers while programming. You also learned how to display numbers and other data in various formats.

This will help you understand how numbers are calculated by your computer, as well as how to enter number values into your program.

In the next chapter, you'll learn how to create, save, and edit disk files using C programming commands.

Working with Files

In This Chapter

Up to this point, we've worked with programs that use your computer's RAM, or *random access memory*. This lets your program work in the temporary area of memory, then disappear or exit from memory when the program is finished.

In this chapter, you'll learn how to work with programs that handle disk file information. Disks are considered long-term memory and let you save data you want to keep for longer than one working session.

File Basics

Disk files are the basic units you work with in the DOS environment. In fact, DOS stands for *disk operating system*. This is an important concept because the only purpose for using disks is to hold program and data files until you want to use them.

You should know a little more about disks if you want to understand files. Disks are considered *long-term memory*, memory which remains intact regardless of whether your computer is turned on or off. You can contrast disk memory with RAM, or *random access memory*, which is considered *short-term memory*. RAM is available only when your computer is turned on. When you turn your computer off, you lose everything that's stored in RAM. RAM is faster than disk memory, but it is not permanent.

Up to this point in the book, you've worked with C commands that manipulate data stored in RAM. Sometimes this data has been stored in RAM by the program, such as when you define variables. At other times, you've loaded data into RAM yourself, such as when you enter your age in years for AGE.EXE or the city name in CITY.EXE.

In this chapter, you'll learn how to work with C commands that handle disk file data. The following are five basic things you can do with disk files:

160

1. Create new files.
2. Open existing files.
3. Write characters to open files.
4. Read characters to open files.
5. Close open files.

The two basic types of files in DOS are text files and binary files. Text files are the type of file you create when you write C code using a text editor or word processor. Binary files are the type of file you create when you compile your C code into executable files. (Actually, your C compiler creates these files.)

Your work with disk files in this book will be limited to text files. Text files are simpler than binary files. The best way to visualize a text file is to view it as a string of characters attached to a file name. You might be able to understand this more clearly when you compare text files to binary files.

Whenever you want to work with a text file, such as when you want to write or read a letter in a word processor (or view C code in your text editor), you must first load your word processing program in your computer's RAM. You do this by typing the file name for the program (**WP** for WordPerfect, **WORD** for Microsoft Word) and pressing Enter. This sends your computer searching for the appropriate file on disk. When your computer finds the file, it loads the program into your computer's memory.

Once your word processor is loaded into RAM, you then tell it to load the contents of the letter you want to view. You use the letter file name to do this. Your word processor looks on your disk for the text file's first byte (using the file name). If it finds the file, it reads as much of the file as it can into your computer's RAM. With a letter, this usually means it reads the entire letter into RAM all the way to the end-of-file marker. In DOS, this is ^ Z, the control code assigned to the letter Z.

What you've done is load a binary file into your computer's memory, which then handles the text file. Although you might know all this already, it's important that you understand these steps, so that you can duplicate them in this chapter. In this chapter you'll create small binary files (written in C) that handle text files. In a way, you'll be duplicating some of the procedures you use when you work with a word processing program.

161

Disk File Input/Output

All your work with disk files involves two procedures: *input* and *output*. Output means putting characters into a file and saving the characters to disk; input means reading a disk file and sending the characters to a device, such as viewing them on your screen, printing them, or sending them through your modem. These two procedures can be referred to as *I/O* (input/output), or *disk I/O*.

There are two levels of disk I/O in ANSI C: *high level* and *low level*. Low level does not mean less sophisticated. In fact, low-level disk I/O is much more complex than high-level disk I/O. Because of this complexity, we're going to work with only high-level I/O in this book. Low-level I/O requires too much work for a beginning programmer, and it's not necessary for routine disk file work.

The primary difference between high-level and low-level disk I/O is the fact that you work with a *buffer* when you work with high-level commands. This buffer is a section of your computer's RAM that's reserved for storing characters. When a group of characters is read into the buffer and stored there, you can access these characters much more quickly. Later, when you save your work, the program will write the characters from the buffer back to the appropriate disk file.

When you work with low-level disk I/O commands, you read and write each character one at a time directly from the disk file. Although there are situations in which this procedure is more advantageous than using a buffer, you won't run into such situations until your programming skills reach the intermediate level.

Common C Disk File Commands

The following four commands comprise the most basic glossary for high-level disk I/O in ANSI C.

fopen()   Finds a file, opens the file, and places a pointer at the first character in the file.

fclose()   Closes the file you are using.

fgetc()   Reads a single character from the file.

fputc()   Puts a single character into a file.

You'll learn how to work with these commands in the rest of this chapter.

The *fopen* Command

Before you can work with a file, you must either create a new file or open an existing file. You do both of these with the `fopen()` command.

The basic syntax for this command is as follows:

```
fopen("filename", mode);
```

The command is `fopen`. The file name is the name you give the new file, or the name of an existing file you want to open. The mode signifies what you want to do with the file. There are 12 modes, as shown in Table 11.1.

Table 11.1. Twelve file modes.

Mode	Meaning
a	Appends text to a file.
a+	Appends a text file for reading or writing.
a+b	Appends a binary file for reading or writing.
ab	Appends to a binary file.
r	Opens a text file for reading.
r+	Opens a text file for reading or writing.
r+b	Opens a binary file for reading or writing.
rb	Opens a binary file for reading.
w	Creates a text file for writing.
w+	Creates a text file for reading or writing.
w+b	Creates a binary file for reading or writing.
wb	Creates a binary file for writing.

163

These modes are *mnemonic* codes that determine what you want to do with a file after you've opened it. For example, the w mode prepares you to write to a file, whereas the r mode reads characters from an existing file. You'll learn how to use these modes later in this chapter.

Before you can actually use the fopen() command, however, you must first declare a variable using the following basic syntax:

```
FILE *pointer
```

The first element, FILE, is a new type of data that points to the file you want to work with using the variable pointer. The asterisk before the variable name pointer indicates that this variable is in fact a *pointer*. This particular type of pointer variable is sometimes called a *stream pointer* because it works with a stream of characters.

This variable definition introduces you to two new concepts in C programming: pointers and streams. The next section describes what these things are.

Pointers and Streams

You don't need to know much about pointers and streams to begin programming in C. But sooner or later you'll have to master the concepts if you want to advance your skills with C. This section is designed to introduce you to pointers and streams without burdening you with unnecessary details.

A pointer has all sorts of meanings in the world of computing. It can refer to a mouse or some other device you use to "point" at items on your screen. It can refer to the screen cursor on a Macintosh computer. In database management, it can refer to an address that identifies the location of a specific database record.

For our use in C programming, we'll define the term *pointer* to mean a variable that refers to a current item. In this case, the current item is a file or a file name.

164

The term *stream* is a bit easier to understand. A stream can be visualized as a stream of characters or a moving string of characters. Characters are read from the contents of a text file in a stream into the buffer. Later, when you save your work, the characters are read in a stream back to the disk file. The full concept of a stream is a bit more complicated than this, but that's all you need to know for your work with files.

The best way to get started working with files is to read characters from a file that already exists on disk. After that, you'll learn how to close the file. Then you'll learn how to create a new file and write characters into it.

Reading Files

To read the contents of a file that already exists on disk, you need to write a program that will locate and open the file, then read a stream of characters to a buffer in RAM, and then display the stream on your screen.

When you want to read characters in a file, you need to use the following two items: the `r` mode and the `fgetc()` function.

You'll insert the r mode in your fopen() function, which looks like the following:

```
fopen("filename", "r");
```

The r mode lets you read characters from the file called filename.

The fgetc() function operates in a way that *gets characters* from the disk file specified as part of the function. The fgetc() function has the following basic syntax.

```
fgetc(variable filename)
```

You can see how these two commands are used in the code for READ.C. Type the contents of this program into a text file.

```
/* READ.C */
/* Reads characters from a disk file */
#include <stdio.h>

main()
{
FILE *file;
char read;

file = fopen("read.c", "r");

while(read != EOF) {
    read = fgetc(file);
    printf("%c", read);
    }
}
```

165

Once you've entered this program code, save the file to disk and compile the program, then run it.

Type **READ**.
Press Enter.

You should see the contents of the text file READ.C displayed on your screen, as shown in Figure 11.1.

```
C:\>read
/* READ.C */
/* Reads characters from a disk file */
#include <stdio.h>

main()
{
FILE *file;
char read;

file = fopen("read.c", "r");

while(read != EOF) {
    read = fgetc(file);
    printf("%c", read);
    }
}
C:\>
```

166

Figure 11.1. Results of running READ.C.

A Closer Look at READ.C

Let's take a closer look at the contents of READ.C. First, you declare two variables, the file pointer variable FILE *file and a variable char read, which you'll use in a while loop.

You then use the file pointer file along with the fopen() function to open the file you want to work with and prepare for how you want to work with it. In this case, the file is READ.C, and you want to read its contents, hence the r mode.

You could read the contents of any other text file in the current directory by inserting the appropriate file name in place of read.c.

The commands in the while loop do the actual file reading. The while loop condition states that the variable read does not equal (!=) EOF. EOF means *end-of-file*—the ^Z or ASCII control code Z character—which denotes the end of all text files. Running across a ^Z character stops the loop.

The second and third statements in the `while` loop do the actual work of reading the file. The first statement uses the `fgetc()` function to read the contents of the file whose name is specified between parentheses. The `fopen()` function already declared the file name to be `read.c`.

The second statement prints each character to screen that's read into the `read` variable.

```
The code is processed this way.
```

The file name `read.c` is searched for, and when found, the program prepares to read its contents. The cycle of commands is set up for reading the file, and the contents are then read and displayed on screen, until the program runs across the ^Z character. This character terminates all text files in DOS. When the ^Z is encountered, the program stops and you're returned to the DOS prompt.

167

Writing Characters

Before you can read characters in a file, you must write them to a file. You learned how to read characters before learning to write them for two reasons. First, it's easier to understand how to read characters. Second, you run a risk when you try to write to a file.

Writing characters to a file can be viewed as the opposite of reading characters from a file, except for one important distinction. The `w` mode, which signifies writing to a file, only writes to a new file. It doesn't add characters to an existing file. (To add characters to an existing file, you must use the `a` mode, which lets you append characters.) Each time you use the `w` mode, you create a file for the first time. If a file exists using the same name you've declared along with the `w` mode, then the first file will be deleted.

When you want to write characters to a file, you need to use these two items: the `w` mode and the `fputc()` function.

You'll insert the `r` mode in your `fopen()` function, as follows:

```
fopen("filename", "w");
```

The w mode creates a file using the filename you specify, then prepares to let you read characters into the file.

The `fputc()` function operates in a way that *puts characters* into a disk file. The `fputc()` function has the following basic syntax.

```
fputc(variable filename)
```

You can see how these two commands are used in the code for WRITE.C. Type the contents of this program into a text file.

```
/* WRITE.C */
/* Writes characters to a file on disk */
#include <stdio.h>

main()
{

FILE *file;
char write;

file = fopen("test","w");
    printf("\nStart typing: ");

while(write != '.') {
    scanf("%c", &write);
    fputc(write, file);
    }
}
```

The construction of this program is similar to READ.C with a few minor differences. We'll take a closer look at them after you run and then test the program.

Once you've written the code for WRITE.C, save it to disk, compile the program. and run it.

Type **WRITE**.
Press Enter.

Your screen should display the instruction start typing:.

Type **This is a BIG test.**

It's important that you enter a period (.) at the end of the text you type.

Press Enter.

This should stop the program and return you to your DOS prompt.

To see whether the program worked or not, first make sure that you're working in the directory containing the program WRITE.C. You'll use the DOS command TYPE to run the test.

Type **TYPE TEST**.

Press Enter.

Your screen should change to look something like that shown in Figure 11.2.

```
C:\>write

Start typing: This is a BIG test.

C:\>type test
This is a BIG test.
C:\>
```

Figure 11.2. Contents of the TEST file.

169

If you see the characters displayed in Figure 11.2, then the program has worked successfully. If you don't see these characters, or you see only a few of them, double check your source code for WRITE.C, then recompile the program and run it again. Remember: It's important that you enter a period (.) at the end of the text you enter.

A Closer Look at WRITE.C

Now let's take a closer look at the source code for WRITE.C. As with READ.C, you declare the same two variables FILE *file and char write.

Use the fopen() function to declare the file name you want to create, and use the w mode. In this case, we're using the file name test without an extension. Most file names should retain an extension, such as test.txt or test.doc. We're not using an extension in this case because it's easier to enter a file name without an extension.

The printf() statement following the fopen() statement displays the message on your screen, Start typing:.

The while loop that follows reads the characters you enter from your keyboard and inserts them into the file called test. This is how it works. First, the condition is set up that writing to the file should continue only as long as the program doesn't run across a period. That's why it's so important that you end the line of text you want to insert in the file with a period. As soon as you type a period, the program stops running. When you insert a period, the condition for the while loop becomes false, and the loop stops.

The scanf() statement reads each character you insert from the keyboard, then writes it to the variable write.

The fputc() statement takes each character in the write variable and puts it into the file created by the file variable.

The process stops when you insert a period. You'll see how this works when you test WRITE.C. The program stops when you press Enter.

Testing WRITE.C

There are two aspects of writing to a file that you ought to test. The first is that the w mode erases any file that exists with the same name you want to write to. The second is that typing a period stops inserting characters into the file.

To run the first test, make sure the file TEST contains some characters.

Type **TYPE TEST**.

Press Enter.

If it doesn't contain any characters, run the WRITE.EXE program and enter some characters into TEST. You can repeat the example given just before Figure 11.2. Make sure that you're familiar with the TEST file contents by running the DOS command TYPE again.

Now run WRITE.EXE, but don't place any text into the TEST file. Just insert a period and press Enter to stop the program.

Type **WRITE**.

Press Enter.

Type **.**

Press Enter.

Now check the contents of TEST.

Type **TYPE TEST**.

Press Enter.

The only thing you should see is a period. All the previous contents were erased when you entered the single period.

The second test you want to run is whether typing a period actually ends the writing to the file.

Type **WRITE**.

Press Enter.

Type **This is a test. Does inserting a period stop writing?**

Press Enter.

When your DOS prompt appears, do the following:

Type **TYPE TEST**.

Press Enter.

Your screen should look like Figure 11.3.

```
C:\>write

Start typing: .

C:\>type test
.
C:\>write

Start typing: This is a test. Does inserting a period stop writing?

C:\>type test
This is a test.
C:\>
```

Figure 11.3. Results of testing WRITE.EXE.

As you can see, all the text you typed after the period was not saved to the file. When the `while` loop ran across the period, it stopped writing the characters to the file TEST.

If, while running WRITE.EXE, you press Enter without typing a period first, your cursor will move down one line and onto the left margin. You can still insert characters. All you've done is insert a hard carriage return into the text file. You must type a period and then press Enter to stop inserting characters.

Appending Characters

You can add or append characters to an existing file using the `a` mode. Appending characters is almost the same as writing characters. The only difference is that when you *write* characters to a file, they are always added to the beginning of the file, erasing all previous characters. When you *append* characters, you add them to the end of the characters in the existing file and preserve all existing characters.

Type the code for APPEND.C to see how appending works. You should notice these three differences:

1. You declare a variable called append rather than write. You could continue to use the write variable if you want. We renamed the variable so that you could visualize how it applies throughout the program.
2. You substitute a for w in the `fopen()` statement. This is the only substantive change in the program code.
3. You change the text in the message that appears on screen— an insignificant change.

```
/* APPEND.C */
/* Adds characters to an existing file */
#include <stdio.h>

main()
{

FILE *file;
char append;

file = fopen("test", "a");
    printf("\nAdd this to file TEST: ");

while(append != '.') {
     scanf("%c",&append);
     fputc(append, file);
    }
}
```

173

Once you've typed this code, save it to disk, compile the program, then run it.

Type **APPEND**.

Press Enter.

Type **This is the second test.**

Remember, you must insert a period for the program to stop accepting characters.

Press Enter.

Now check the contents of TEST.

Type **TYPE TEST**.
Press Enter.

Your screen should change to look something like Figure 11.4.

```
C:\>append

Add this to file TEST: This is the second test.

C:\>type test
This is a test.This is the second test.
C:\>
```

Figure 11.4. Results of running APPEND.EXE.

The first part of the file TEST might be a bit different from that shown in Figure 11.4, because you may have changed some text when you tested WRITE.EXE in the previous section.

When you append characters to a file, you're not given the luxury of adding characters wherever you want to in the file. You have to write more sophisticated code to do this.

Closing Files

Up to this point, you've learned how to read the contents of text file, write characters to a new file, and append characters to an existing file. All these programs have been very simple. The one thing you haven't done, however, is close the files. This doesn't make much of a difference with the simple programs you've been writing, but you should learn how to close files correctly so that you can make a habit of it. When you start to read and write different files in the same program, you'll begin to bump into file conflicts if files aren't opened and closed in the correct manner.

To close a file, use the `fclose()` function, whose basic syntax looks is as follows:

```
fclose(filename)
```

The following code shows how and where you would insert this function in the program APPEND.C.

```
/* APPEND.C */
/* Adds characters to an existing file */
#include <stdio.h>

main()
{

FILE *file;
char append;

file = fopen("test", "a");

  printf("\nAdd this to file TEST: ");
  while(append != '.') {
    scanf("%c",&append);
    fputc(append,file);
    }
fclose(file);
}
```

175

The last statement, `fclose(file);`, closes the file name attached to the `file` variable using the `fopen()` function.

A Common Security Message

When you start with the simple programs in this chapter, you probably won't make a mistake specifying which file name you want to use. But as your work becomes more sophisticated, it's possible that the file name you specify does not exist, or does not exist where you think it does. It would be helpful to insert enough commands to tell you when the program can't find the file you've specified. (These sorts of commands needn't be complicated. They should just alert you to a situation that's developed which prevents the program from operating the way its supposed to.)

You can use the following if loop to check whether the file you specify can be found.

```
if(file == NULL) {
   printf("Cannot find the file you specify!");
   exit();

}
```

When the fopen() function can't find the specified file name, it will return a NULL value. The condition of this loop states that when the file name equals NULL, the security message should be printed, then the program will exit.

If you insert this security message into READ.C, it would look like the following:

```
/* READ.C */
/* Reads characters from a disk file */
#include <stdio.h>

main()
{
FILE *file;
char read;

file = fopen("xyz", "r");

if(file == NULL) {
   printf("Couldn't find the file you specified!");
   exit();
   }

while(read != EOF) {
   read = fgetc(file);
   printf("%c", read);
   }
fclose(file);
}
```

If you look closely at this code, you'll see that we changed the file name from test to xyz. If you save, compile, and run this program, you should see the message shown in Figure 11.5 on your screen.

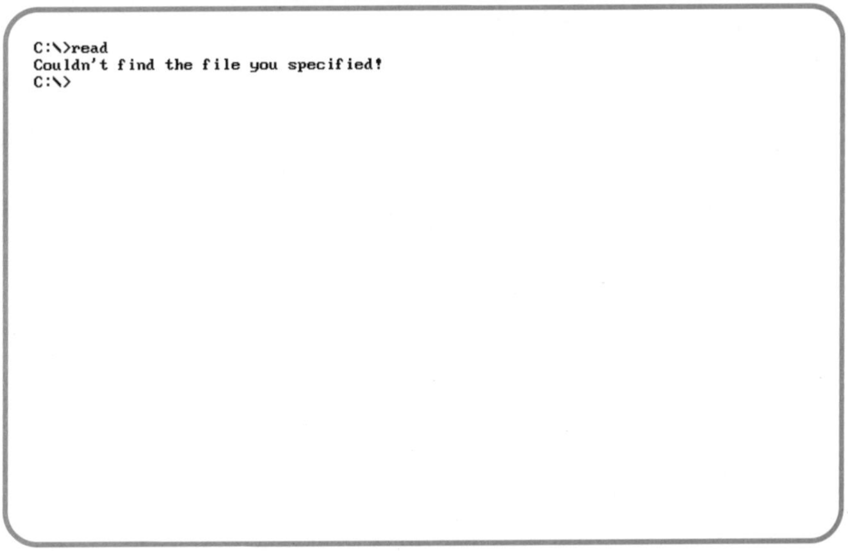

```
C:\>read
Couldn't find the file you specified!
C:\>
```

Figure 11.5. Results of running READ.C with a security message.

You have to use READ.C for the security message, because if you use WRITE.C or APPEND.C, a new file XYZ will be created when the program doesn't find a file with that name.

Summary

In this chapter, you learned how to work with files using C programming terms. File work is extremely important in C because files are important to DOS, and files contain all the instructions and data you need to perform your work on a computer.

This concludes your introduction to the C programming language. You should review information provided in the following appendixes, so that you can remember more clearly the lessons you learned in this book. You can also use the information to expand on your knowledge of C.

If you want to continue your education with C, you should take a look at *The Waite Group's Microsoft C Bible, 2nd Ed.* (SAMS) and *The Waite Group's Microsoft C Programming for the PC, 2nd Ed.* (SAMS) for more information.

178

Popular C Programs

In This Appendix

Although there is a variety of versions of the C programming language for all sorts of computer systems, the only version that interests us in this book is the ANSI version for IBM PCs.

C Programming Language Environments

In the current market, six proprietary C language applications are used by most programmers:

▶ Turbo C++, manufactured by Borland International.

▶ Turbo C++ Professional, manufactured by Borland International.

▶ Borland C++, manufactured by Borland International—an enhanced version of Turbo C++.

- ▶ QuickC, manufactured by Microsoft Corporation.
- ▶ Microsoft C Compiler, manufactured by Microsoft Corporation.
- ▶ Watcom C, manufactured by Watcom Products, Inc.

Because of the fierce competition for C language products, these programs are being revised continuously, with new versions coming out yearly. You should ascertain which version is current before you buy or upgrade your current version.

All these programs provide an editor with which the user can insert C code as text commands and save the C code to disk. These programs also provide a compiler for converting the C code to machine-readable code, a linker, and a library of functions and additional files that can be used to enhance your work building programs.

You can also obtain debugger programs from Borland International (Turbo Debugger) and Microsoft Corporation (CodeView) that help you debug your programs. Debugging is a sophisticated activity. For the type of work you're going to do in this book, you probably won't need to use a debugger. In most cases, when you run across a problem, you'll be able to figure out what's wrong by taking a second look at the program code. None of our programs will extend beyond a handful of lines of code, so it's easy to double check your work against the examples provided in the book.

The rest of this appendix is devoted to details about the two most popular C language programs on the market for beginners: Turbo C++ from Borland International and QuickC from Microsoft Corp.

180

Turbo C++

Turbo C++ is the original name of the C language programming environment manufactured by Borland International. This package comes in three forms: Borland C++, which is the professional environment; Turbo C++, which is completely sufficient to generate professional level C program code, but which doesn't contain some of the advanced elements of Borland C++; and Turbo C++ Professional, which is Turbo C++ with Turbo Debugger, Turbo Assembler, and Turbo Profiler.

Installing Turbo C++

The Turbo C++ program disks come in two forms: eight disks measuring 5.25" or four disks measuring 3.5".

You can install Turbo C++ very easily following these steps:

1. Locate the disk marked Disk 1 (from either the 3.5" set of disks or the 5.25" set of disks).
2. Place Disk 1 in your A drive.
3. Type **A:** and press Enter to log onto your A drive.
4. Type **INSTALL** and press Enter to begin the installation process.

When the first screen appears, press Enter twice to view the recommended directory structure for the program. This screen looks like Figure A.1.

181

```
                    ┌─────────────────────────────────┐
                    │ Turbo C++ Installation Utility  │
                    └─────────────────────────────────┘

   ┌────────────────────────────────────────────────────────────┐
   │ Turbo C++ Directory:          C:\TC                         │
   │ Binary Files Subdirectory:    C:\TC\BIN                     │
   │ Header Files Subdirectory:    C:\TC\INCLUDE                 │
   │ Library Subdirectory:         C:\TC\LIB                     │
   │ BGI Subdirectory:             C:\TC\BGI                     │
   │ Tour Subdirectory:            C:\TC\TOUR                    │
   │ Class Library Subdirectory:   C:\TC\CLASSLIB               │
   │ Examples Subdirectory:        C:\TC\EXAMPLES               │
   │ Install Tour:                 Yes                           │
   │ Unpack Examples:              Yes                           │
   │ Memory Models...              [ S M C L H ]                 │
   │                                                             │
   │ Start Installation                                          │
   └────────────────────────────────────────────────────────────┘
   ───────────────────────── Description ─────────────────────────
    Press ENTER to change the directory in which to place the Turbo C++
    executable files and system files.  This includes the configuration files
    and the help file.
   F1-Help  F9-Start the installation  ENTER-Select  ESC-Previous
```

Figure A.1. The recommended directory structure for Turbo C++.

The installation program for Turbo C++ is a full-screen, menu-driven program. All you need to do is read the questions on each screen and answer the questions that configure the system the way you want.

When all the files from the first disk have been installed, you'll be asked to replace Disk 1 with Disk 2. The Install program will walk you through all seven disks this way.

When you've finished installing all program files for Turbo C++, your version of the program will be installed in a series of subdirectories that look like the following:

```
TC
    BIN
    INCLUDE
        SYS
    LIB
    BGI
    TOUR
    CLASSLIB
        EXAMPLES
        INCLUDE
        LIB
        SOURCE
    EXAMPLES
        TCCALC
        STARTUP
```

You can find the main program file, TC.EXE, in the BIN directory. You should probably place this directory on your path, as described later in this appendix.

You can now run Turbo C++ to see what it's like.

Test Run Turbo C++

Once you've installed all the files for Turbo C++, you should make sure that the program loads into your computer. Follow these steps to check the program:

1. Type **C:** (that's the letter *C* or *c* followed by a colon), then press Enter. This ensures that you're logged onto the C drive. (Or type the letter of the drive you used to contain the Turbo C++ program files.)

2. Type **CD** and press Enter to make sure you're logged onto the root directory.

3. Type **CD TC\BIN** and press Enter to log onto the Turbo C++ BIN directory.

4. Type **TC** and press Enter to load the Turbo C++ program.

If the program is loaded correctly, you'll see the program copyright screen appear momentarily, followed by the Turbo C++ editing screen, which looks like Figure A.2.

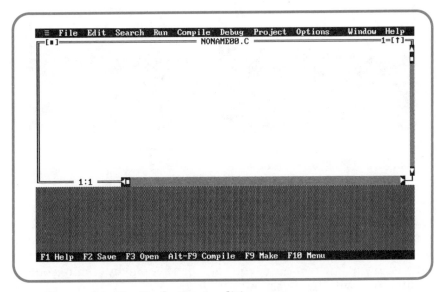

Figure A.2. The Turbo C++ editing screen.

You can enter text characters into this screen using the standard text editing keys. Press the characters keys (letters, numbers and punctuation marks) to insert characters, press Enter to insert a carriage return, and so on.

Turbo C++ is a menu-driven program. That is, you can execute the most commonly used commands using menus that pull down from the top menu bar.

To use the menu system, press F10 or the Alt key and then the letter of the menu you want to use. For example, to edit your C program text, press F10-F, and the File menu will appear, as shown in Figure A.3.

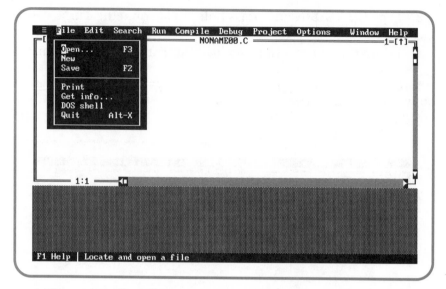

Figure A.3. The File menu open in Turbo C++.

184

For some users, it's easier to press Alt and the menu letter. You can also open menus by pressing F10 to activate the top menu bar, press the right arrow key or the left arrow key to highlight the name of the menu you want to use, then press Enter to open the menu. Finally, if you have a mouse, you can open a menu by clicking on the menu name with the left mouse button.

To use commands on a menu, press the letter highlighted in the command you want to use. For example, to execute the Open command on the edit menu, press **O**. This opens the Load file window, which lets you create a new file or open an existing file.

To cancel opening a file, press Esc. Pressing Esc always backs you out of where you're going and returns you to the previous level.

Notice how the Open command on the File menu is duplicated by the function key F3. To see how this works, close the File menu by pressing Esc. Now press F3. This opens the Load file window directly.

You can also execute menu commands by highlighting the menu command by pressing the down arrow or the up arrow. Then press Enter to execute the command.

Help!

Borland programs are famous for their interactive, context-sensitive help. If you need help at any location in the program, just press F1. If you do this when the edit screen is showing, you'll be given the information shown in Figure A.4.

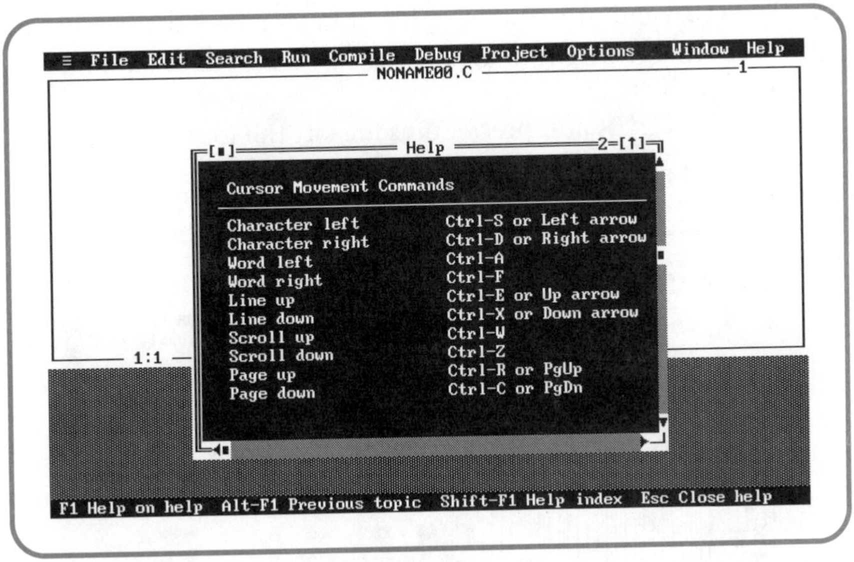

Figure A.4. Help screen in Turbo C++.

You can scroll up and down most Help windows for more information by pressing PgDn or PgUp. To close a Help window, press Esc.

Quitting the Program

To exit Turbo C++, press Alt-X. This returns you to your DOS prompt. If you have any unsaved work, Turbo C++ will ask whether you want to save or abandon your unsaved changes, and then it lets you exit.

You can also exit Turbo C++ by pressing F10-F-X.

Taking a Tour

The Turbo C++ program can give you a guided tour using the file called TCTOUR.EXE. If you've never used Turbo C++ before, you should probably take this tour.

To take the Turbo C++ tour:

1. Type **CD** and press Enter to log onto your root directory.
2. Type **CD TC\TOUR** to log onto the directory that contains the tour files.
3. Type **TCTOUR** and press Enter to start the tour.

The first screen of the tour looks like Figure A.5.

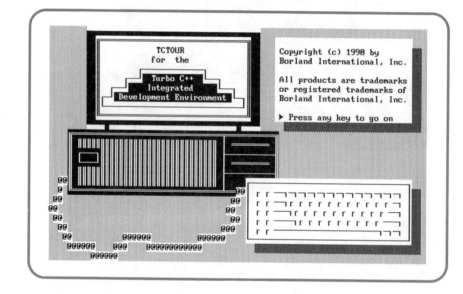

Figure A.5. First screen of the Turbo C++ tour.

Press Enter several times to walk through the first few screens. The program will ask you to configure the tour for a color or black-and-white screen. It will also ask you your name. You can walk through the tour from beginning to end, select different parts to view, or exit the tour by pressing Q (for Quit) at various points in the tour.

Installing Turbo C++ on Your Path

Once you've installed Turbo C++ on your hard disk, you should place that BIN directory on your path. This is the directory that contains the main program file TC.EXE.

To place C:\TC\BIN on your path, open your AUTOEXEC.BAT file. Figure A.6 shows what a sample AUTOEXEC.BAT file looks like when viewed in the PC Tools PC Shell editor.

```
PCTOOLS V6  Desktop  File  Edit  Search  Controls  Window        1 28 pm
                            === Notepad ===
 Line: 5     Col: 34                                      autoexec.bat INS
 @echo off
 break on
 verify on
 prompt=$p$g
 path=c:\;c:\dos;c:\wp;c:\pctools;




 1Help  2Index  3Exit  4Load  5Save  6Find  7Spell  8      9Swap  10Menu
```

Figure A.6. Sample AUTOEXEC.BAT file.

Enter the following information somewhere in your path statement:

```
C:\TC\BIN;
```

Now the sample AUTOEXEC.BAT file shown in Figure A.6 should change to look like that shown in Figure A.7.

187

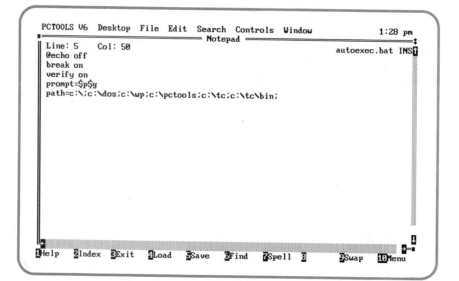

Figure A.7. Sample AUTOEXEC.BAT modified.

QuickC

QuickC is one of two C language programming environments manufactured by Microsoft Corporation, the makers of the PC DOS and MS-DOS operating systems.

QuickC is the easier of the two Microsoft C language programs to use, and the less sophisticated. It's designed for first-time programmers.

Installing QuickC

When you open your QuickC package, you'll find the program files on four 5.25" disks marked Setup, Learning, Utilities/Compiler, and Libraries.

If you want to install the program from 3.5" disks, you should fill out a card for such purposes enclosed in the package, then send the card to Microsoft Corporation.

To load the QuickC program files from 5.25" disks:

1. Locate the disk marked "Setup."
2. Place it in your A drive.
3. Type **A:** and press Enter to log onto your A drive.
4. Type **SETUP** and press Enter to begin the installation process.

When the first screen appears, you'll be given certain information about the program and the installation process, as shown in Figure A.8.

```
Microsoft (R) QuickC (R) with QuickAssembler Setup Program, Version 2.51
Copyright (C) Microsoft Corp. 1986-90.  All rights reserved.




------
IMPORTANT: If you have not already read the information on the SETUP program in
your Microsoft QuickC (R) 2.5 Up and Running manual, please do so before
continuing with the installation process.  This document, in addition to the
README.DOC on the SETUP disk, contains important information regarding the use
of this program.

If you are unsure of the proper reply for any of these questions, consider the
defaults as a good place to start.  If you later find that you would have
preferred to make other choices, you can always run SETUP again.

If you make a mistake during the setup process you can type CTRL+C to quit at
any time and run the program again.  SETUP never erases files from the
distribution disks.
------
Press <ENTER> to continue or Q to quit:
```

Figure A.8. First QuickC screen.

You should press Enter several times to move into the installation process. Most of the questions the Install program asks you are already answered with defaults surrounded by brackets, as follows: [Y] for yes, [N] for no. You should probably accept the default replies until you become more adept with QuickC.

There's only one question for which you should change the answer. At the bottom of several screens, after displaying a list of installation choices, the Install program will ask: Do you want to change any of the above options? [Y]. In this case, type **N** and press Enter. If you accept the default answer [Y] for yes, you'll be given the options all over again so that you can change them.

Once you've finished installing the files from the first disk, you'll be asked to replace the Setup disk with the Utilities/Compiler disk. The Install program will walk you through all four disks this way.

After installing all the program files, the Install program will proceed to build Turbo C++ libraries. Once this is done, you can answer more questions (by pressing Enter to accept the defaults), then press Enter one final time to exit the Install program.

When the QuickC program is fully installed, it will have created a directory structure for the program files that looks like the following:

```
QC25
    BIN
    LIB
    INCLUDE
        SYSTEM
```

You can now run QuickC to see what it's like. If you plan to use QuickC often, you should consider putting the QuickC BIN directory in your path statement. This is described later in this appendix.

Test Run Quick C

Once you've installed QuickC on your hard disk, you can run the program to make sure that it loads correctly.

To load the QuickC program:

1. Type **C:** and press Enter to make sure that you're logged onto the C drive (or whatever drive you used to contain the QuickC program files).
2. Type **CD** and press Enter to make sure that you're logged onto the root directory.
3. Type **CD QC25\BIN** and press Enter to log onto the QuickC BIN directory.
4. Type **QC** and press Enter to load the QuickC program.

When the program is fully loaded, it will display the editing screen, as shown in Figure A.9.

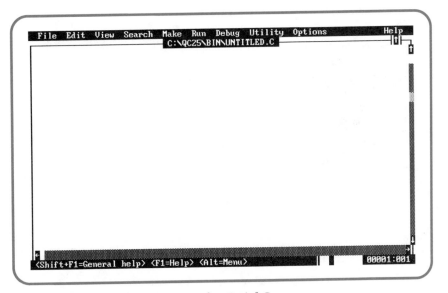

Figure A.9. Editing screen for QuickC.

You can enter text characters into this screen using the standard text-editing keys. Press the keys (letters, numbers, and punctuation marks) to insert characters, press Enter to insert a carriage return, and so on.

QuickC is a menu-driven program. This means that you can execute the most commonly used commands using menus that pull down from the top menu bar.

To use the menu system, press F10 or the Alt key and then the letter of the menu you want to use. For example, to edit your C program text, press F10-F, and the File menu will appear, as shown in Figure A.10.

For some users, it's easier to press Alt and the menu letter. You can also open menus by pressing F10 to activate the top menu bar, then press the right arrow key or the left arrow key to highlight the name of the menu you want to use. Then press Enter to open the menu.

To use commands on a menu, press the letter highlighted in the command you want to use. For example, to execute the `Open` command on the edit menu, press **O**. This opens the window that lets you create a new file or open an existing file.

To cancel opening a file, press Esc. Pressing Esc backs you out of where you're going and returns you to the previous level.

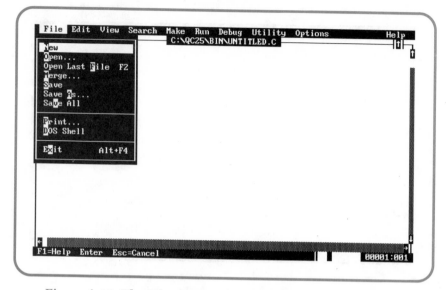

Figure A.10. The File menu open in QuickC.

You can also execute menu commands by highlighting the menu command. Press the down arrow key or the up arrow key, then press Enter to execute the command.

Help!

The QuickC program provides two types of help: general and specific help. You can always open the general Help screen by pressing Shift-F1. This opens the screen shown in Figure A.11.

To close this and other Help screens, press Esc.

The second type of help is called specific help, because it provides help for specific features in the QuickC program. You press F1 to access this help. For example, to find out more about the Files pull-down menu, open that menu first by pressing Alt-F. Once the menu is open, press F1 and you'll see the screen shown in Figure A.12.

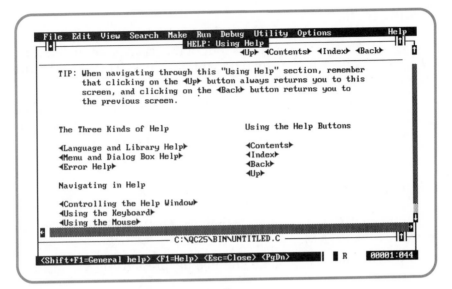

Figure A.11. The general Help screen for QuickC.

193

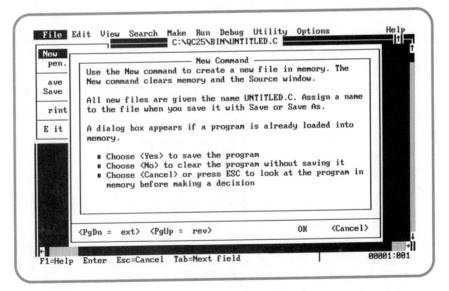

Figure A.12. Help specific to the File pull-down menu.

Taking a Tour

The QuickC program provides a tour of the basic program features. The tour is built-in to the program. You can access it using the Utility pull-down menu.

To begin the tour, press Alt-U to open the Utility menu, then press L to execute the `Learn QuickC` command. You can follow the tour as far as you want, then bail out at any point.

Quitting QuickC

To quit Quick C, the shortcut is to press Alt-F4. This will take you directly back to DOS.

If you want to use menu commands, press Alt-F-X.

Installing QuickC on Your Path

Once you've installed QuickC on your hard disk, you should place the BIN directory on your path. This is the directory that contains the main program file QC.EXE.

To place C:\QC25\BIN on your path, open your AUTOEXEC.BAT file. Figure A.13 shows what a sample AUTOEXEC.BAT file looks like when viewed in the PC Tools PC Shell editor.

Enter the following information somewhere in your path statement:

```
C:\QC25\BIN;
```

Now the sample AUTOEXEC.BAT file shown in Figure A.13 should change to look like that shown in Figure A.14.

That's all there is to it. Once you've installed a C programming environment on your disk, you're ready to go to work. You can now jump back to Chapter 1 and prepare to start writing your first C program.

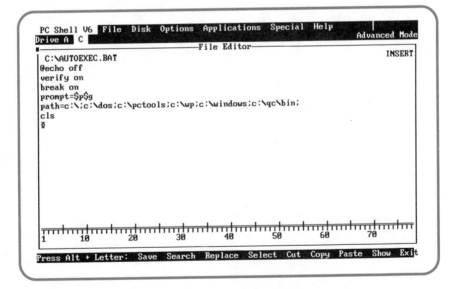

Figure A.13. Sample AUTOEXEC.BAT file.

195

Figure A.14. Sample AUTOEXEC.BAT modified.

ANSI C Keywords

In This Appendix

There are 32 keywords in the ANSI standard of the C language. These keywords must always be written in lowercase.

Keywords

auto   The default storage class for most function variables. Used to create temporary variables within a block that exist only for the duration of the block.

break   Used to exit from a `do`, `for`, or `while` loop, or to exit from a `switch` statement.

case   A section within a `switch` statement. See `switch` later in this list.

char   A data type for character variables. Represents a single byte.

const	A modifier that tells the C compiler the variable that follows cannot be changed while the program is running.
continue	Forces the conditional test in a loop to be performed, bypassing the rest of the statements in the loop.
default	Used in a switch statement. Signals a block of code that will be executed if no other matches are found in any case statement. See switch later in this list.
do	The first half of a do-while loop, in which the condition is not checked until the end of the loop forcing the statements in the loop to be performed at least one time. See while later in this list.
double	A data type for floating point variables which forces double precision.
else	The second half of an if-else loop. See if later in this list.
enum	Used to create enumeration types. Lets you create a list of objects each with a particular integer value.
extern	Used as a storage class modifier telling the compiler that a variable function has been stored elsewhere in the program.
float	A data type specifier declaring floating point variables.
for	Used to begin a for loop. Checks a condition and increments a counter for each pass in the loop.
goto	Causes the program to jump to a specific label marking a block of code.
if	Used to begin an if conditional loop. Checks a condition. If the condition is true, the associated statement is executed. Can also be used as the first half of an if-else loop, with which an else statement is executed when the if condition is false.

198

int	A data type declaring integer or whole number variables.
long	A data type declaring integer variables that are twice as long as short data type integer variables. See short later in this list.
register	A storage modifier that specifies a variable that should be stored in a register allowing speedy access to the variable.
return	Used to force a return from a function. Yields a value for the function declaration.
short	A data type declaring integer variables that are half as long as long data type integer variables. See long earlier on this list.
signed	A data type declaring signed (– or +) character and integer type variables.
sizeof	Used to return the size of the data object.
static	A data type that tells the compiler to store permanently the local variable that precedes it.
struct	Used to create complex variables.
switch	Used to route execution down one of several branches defined by case definitions. Can include a default definition that executes if no case definition is called.
typedef	Used to create a new name for an existing data type.
union	Used to unite two or more variables at the same memory location.
unsigned	A data type used to eliminate the sign before integer and character type variables.
void	Used to signify a function that returns no value.
volatile	Used to define a variable that can be changed at any point during the program execution.
while	Used to begin a while loop, which checks a condition before it executes a statement.

199

Standard ANSI C Headers

In This Appendix

This appendix is divided into four parts. The first part lists all standard C header files in alphabetical order, defines them, and supplies a list of functions, macros, and type definitions that are controlled by each header file.

The second, third, and fourth parts list all functions, macros, and type definitions in alphabetical order. They show which header file controls the item.

Header Files

Header files let you declare functions and define macros and type definitions within a program.

`assert.h`	Helps diagnose logical errors in a program by defining the macro `assert`.
`ctype.h`	Stands for Character TYPE. Lets you classify character functions using arguments returned from the following character functions: `isalnum, isalpha, iscntrl, isdigit, isgraph, islower, isprint, ispunct, isspace, isupper, isxdigit, tolower,` and `toupper`.
`errno.h`	Stands for ERRor Number. Tests the values stored in `errno` in other library functions. When a program starts out, `errno = 0`. Any library function can change the errno value. See macros: `edom, erange,` and `errno`.
`float.h`	Helps ascertain characteristics of floating type representations.
`limits.h`	Helps ascertain characteristics of integer type representations.
`locale.h`	Lets you change characteristics of the current locale value and adapt to different environments.
`math.h`	Lets you declare functions that perform common mathematical calculations on values of the *double* type. You can obtain two types of error checks with this header: *domain error* and *range error*.
`setjmp.h`	Stands for SET JuMP. Lets you perform `goto` statements that jump normal `call` and `return` commands in a program.
`signal.h`	Stands for SIGNAL. Lets you determine how the program handles `signal` calls while it is running.
`stdarg.h`	Stands for STandarD ARGument. Lets you work with unnamed additional arguments in a function that accepts other arguments of varying length.
`stddef.h`	Stands for STandarD DEFinition. Lets you define several types and macros for general use through your program.

202

`stdio.h`	Stands for STandarD Input Output. Lets you perform basic input and output procedures to your terminal, printer, or disk file.
`stdlib.h`	Stands for STandarD LIBrary. Lets you define other useful functions, macros, and types.
`string.h`	Lets you work with functions that manipulate strings and character arrays.
`time.h`	Lets you declare functions that let you manipulate dates and times.

Functions

Functions determine what actions will occur when a program is run. All functions, when written correctly, return some value to the program. The nature of the function determines what type of information is returned by the function.

203

assert.h

`isalnum`	Returns nonzero if the character is any letter (A-Z, a-z) or decimal number (0-9). These are called alphanumeric characters.
`isalpha`	Returns nonzero if the character is any letter (A-Z, a-z).
`iscntrl`	Returns nonzero if the character is any control character. There are 32 control characters.
`isdigit`	Returns nonzero if the character is any decimal digit (0-9).
`isgraph`	Returns nonzero if the character is a printing character and not a space.
`islower`	Returns nonzero if the character is a lowercase letter (a-z).
`isprint`	Returns nonzero if the character is a printing character (including a space).

ispunct	Returns nonzero if the character is a printing character (isprint) or an alphanumeric character (isalnum).
isspace	Returns nonzero if the character is one of the following six control codes, or a space: CR (carriage return), FF (form feed), HT (hard tab), NL (new line), or VT (vertical tab).
isupper	Returns nonzero if the character is an uppercase letter (A-Z).
isxdigit	Returns nonzero if the character is a hexadecimal number (0-9, A-F, or a-f).
tolower	Returns the lowercase version of a letter if the character is an alphabetic character (A-Z, a-z); otherwise, it returns the original character.
toupper	Returns the uppercase version of a letter if the character is an alphabetic character (A-Z, a-z); otherwise, it returns the original character.

204

locale.h

lconv	Lets you format or convert numeric values.
localeconv	Returns a pointer to a static duration structure containing the numeric formatted information, which cannot be altered.
setlocale	Returns a point to a static duration string describing a new locale; otherwise it returns a null pointer.

math.h

acos	Stands for Angle COSine. Returns the value of the angle whose cosine is x within the range $[0,\pi]$ radians.
asin	Stands for Angle SINe. Returns the value of the angle whose sine is x within the range $-\pi/2, +\pi/2$ radians.

atan	Stands for Angle TANgent. Returns the value of the angle whose tangent is *x* within the range $-\pi/2$, $+\pi/2$ radians.
atan2	Stands for Angle TANgent. Returns the value of the angle whose tangent is *y/x* within the range $-\pi$, $+\pi$ radians.
ceil	Stands for CEILing value. Returns the smallest integer value not less than *x*.
cos	Stands for COSine. Returns the cosine value of *x* for *x* in radians.
cosh	Stands for COSine Hyperbolic. Returns the hyperbolic cosine value of *x*.
exp	Stands for EXPonential. Returns the exponential value of *x*, e^x
fabs	Stands for Function ABSolute. Returns the absolute value of *x*, /x/.
floor	Stands for FLOOR value. Returns the largest integer value not greater than *x*.
fmod	Stands for Function MODe. Returns the remainder of x/y, which is x–i*y for the integer *i*, such that i*y<x<(i+l)*y. If *y*=0, the function returns a domain error, otherwise it returns the value 0.
frexp	Stands for FRaction EXPonent. Returns a fraction value *f* and binary value *i* that represents the value of *x*, then stores the integer *i* in pexp.
ldexp	Stands for Long Double EXPonent. Returns the value $x*2^{exp}$.
log	Stands for LOG. Returns the natural logarithmic value of *x*.
log10	Stands for LOG base 10. Returns the base 10 logarithmic value of *x*.
modf	Stands for MODe Function. Returns the integer *i* plus a fraction value *f*, which represents the value *x*.

205

pow	Stands for POWer. Returns the value of x raised to the power y, x^y.
sin	Stands for SINe. Returns the sine value of x for x in radians.
sinh	Stands for SINe Hyperbolic. Returns the hyperbolic sine value of x.
sqrt	Stands for SQuare RooT. Returns the square root value of x.
tan	Stands for TANgent. Returns the tangent value of x for x in radians.
tanh	Stands for TANgent Hyperbolic. Returns the hyperbolic tangent value for x.

signal.h

raise	Returns the signal sig as well as the value 0 if the signal is reported.
signal	Stands for SIGNAL. Lets you specify a new handling for sig and checks the previous handling.

stdio.h

clearerr	Stands for CLEAR ERrors. Clears the end-of-file and error indicators for stream.
fclose	Stands for File CLOSE. Closes the file associated with stream; otherwise, it returns EOF.
feof	Stands for Function End Of File. Returns a value if the end-of-file indicator is set for stream.
ferror	Stands for Function ERROR. Returns a value if the error indicator is set for stream.
fflush	Stands for File FLUSH. Writes buffered output to the file associated with stream; otherwise, it returns EOF.

`fgetc`	Stands for File GET C. Reads the next character from the `input` stream, moves the file position indicator forward, and returns the character; otherwise, it returns `EOF`.
`fgetpos`	Stands for File GET POSition. Stores the file position indicator for `stream` and returns 0 if successful; otherwise, the function stores the returned value in `errno`.
`fgets`	Stands for File GET Stream. Reads characters from `stream` and stores them in successive elements of an array.
`fopen`	Stands for File OPEN. Opens a file with the specified file name and returns a pointer to the data object controlling the stream.
`fprintf`	Stands for File PRINT Formatted. Outputs formatted text using `format` and writes the characters to `stream`.
`fputc`	Stands for File PUT Character. Outputs a character to `stream`, advances the file position indicator, and returns the output character; otherwise, it returns `EOF`.
`fputs`	Stands for File PUT String. Locates characters in a string and outputs them to `stream`; otherwise, it returns `EOF`.
`fread`	Stands for File READ. Locates characters from the input `stream` and stores them in elements of an array.
`freopen`	Stands for File name REOPEN. Closes the current file associated with `stream`, then opens a specified file name and associates it with the stream; otherwise, it returns a null pointer.
`fscanf`	Stands for File SCAN Formatted text. Scans formatted text using `format`, locates each scanned character in `stream`, then returns the number of items; otherwise, it returns `EOF`.
`fseek`	Stands for File position indicator SEEK. Sets the file position indicator for `stream`, clears the end-of-file indicator, then returns 0 if successful.

207

`fsetpos`	Stands for File SET POSition indicator. Sets the file position indicator for `stream`.
`ftell`	Stands for File TELL. Returns an encoded form of the file position indicator for `stream`.
`fwrite`	Stands for File WRITE. Outputs characters to `stream`.
`getc`	Stands for GET C. Reads the next character from the input `stream`, moves the file position indicator forward, and returns the character; otherwise, it returns `EOF`. Similar to `fgetc` except this can read `stream` more than once.
`getchar`	Stands for GET CHARacter. Reads the next character from the input `stream`, moves the file position indicator forward, and returns the character; otherwise, it returns `EOF`. Identical to `fgetc`.
`gets`	Stands for GET Stream. Reads characters from `stdin` and stores them in an array.
`perror`	Stands for Pointer ERROR. Outputs a line of text to `stderr`.
`printf`	Stands for PRINT Formatted text. Outputs formatted text under `format`.
`putc`	Stands for PUT C. Outputs a character to `stream`, advances the file position indicator, and returns the output character; otherwise, it returns `EOF`. Similar to `fgetc` except this can read `stream` more than once.
`putchar`	Stands for PUT CHARacter. Outputs a character to `stream`, advances the file position indicator, and returns the output character; otherwise, it returns `EOF`. Identical to `fputc`.
`puts`	Stands for PUT String. Locates characters in a string and outputs them to `stdout`.
`remove`	Stands for REMOVE file. Removes the specified file name and returns 0 if successful.
`rename`	Stands for RENAME file. Renames an old file with the specified new file name.

208

rewind	Stands for REWIND stream. Resets the stream.
scanf	Stands for SCAN Formatted text. Scans formattted text under format.
setbuf	Stands for SET BUFfer. Sets the current buffer.
setvbuf	Stands for SET Value BUFfering mode. Sets the buffering mode for stream.
sprintf	Stands for Stores PRINTed Formatted text. Outputs formatted text under format and stores it in an array.
sscanf	Stands for SCANs Formatted text. Scans formatted text under format and stores it in an array.
tmpfile	Stands for TeMPorary binary FILE. Creates a temporary binary file.
tmpnam	Stands for TeMP file NAMe. Creates a temporary file name and returns a pointer to the file name.
ungetc	Stands for UNsigned GET C. Stores C in the data object for stream.
vfprintf	Stands for Value Formatted text PRINT using Format. Outputs formatted text under format and writes characters to stream.
vprintf	Stands for Value PRINT Formatted text. Outputs formatted text under format and writes characters to stdout.
vsprintf	Stands for Value array PRINT Formatted text; this outputs formatted text under format and stores it in an array.

209

stdlib.h

abort	Calls raise, which returns the abort signal.
abs	Returns the absolute value of a number.
atexit	Stands for AT EXIT. Registers the function func to be called by exit and returns 0 if successful.

`atof`	Stands for A TO F. Converts the characters in a string to equivalent *double* value.
`atoi`	Stands for A TO Integer. Converts the characters in a string to an equivalent integer value.
`atol`	Stands for A TO Long. Converts the characters in a string to an equivalent long value.
`bsearch`	Stands for Binary SEARCH. Searches for values and returns their address.
`calloc`	Stands for Character ALLOCation. Allocates an array data object and returns the first address of the array; otherwise, it returns a null pointer.
`div`	Stands for DIVision. Divides two numbers and returns both quotient and remainder.
`exit`	Stands for EXIT. Calls all functions registered by `atexit`, closes all files and returns control to the target environment.
`free`	Stands for FREE data object. Deallocates a data object.
`getenv`	Stands for GET ENVironment. Gets a string by searching an environment list.
`labs`	Stands for Long ABSolute. Returns the absolute value of a number.
`ldiv`	Stands for Long DIVision. Calculates long division and returns both the result and a remainder.
`ldiv_t`	Stands for Long DIVision Type. A structure type that holds the value returned by `ldiv`.
`malloc`	Stands for Make ALLOCation. Allocates a data object of a certain size and returns the address of the data object.
`mblen`	Stands for MultiByte LENgth of a string. Calculates the number of bytes in a string.
`mbstowcs`	Stands for MultiByte String TO address (WCS). Stores a multibyte character string in an array whose first element is at the address wcs.

210

mbtowc	Stands for MultiByte TO next character (WC). Determines the number of characters in a multibyte string that constitute the next multibyte character.
qsort	Stands for SORT. Sorts an array of elements.
rand	Stands for RANDom. Computes a pseudo-random number.
realloc	Stands for REturning address and ALLOCating data. Allocates a data object size and returns the addess.
size_t	Stands for SIZE of operator Type. size_t is the unsigned integer type.
srand	Stands for Seed RANDom number. Stores that seed value used to computer a pseudorandom number.
strtod	Stands for STRing TO Double. Converts the initial characters of a string to an equivalent value of type *double*.
strtol	Stands for STRing TO Long. Converts the initial characters of a string to an equivalent value of type long.
strtoul	Stands for STRing TO Unsigned Long. Converts the initial characters of a string to an equivalent value of type unsigned long.
system	Stands for SYSTEM. Passes a string to be executed to the CPU.
wchar_t	Stands for Wide CHARacter Type integer. Declares a data object type.
wcstombs	Stands for address (WCS) TO MultiByte String. Stores a multibyte string.
wctomb	Stands for WChar TO MultiByte. Determines the number of characters need to represent a multibyte character corresponding to wide character.

211

Macros

Macros are stored in the library of header files. When your program runs across a declared macro, it expands the macro into an expression. The following macros are defined by the expressions they contain.

errno.h

`edom`	Stands for Error DOMain. Returns the value stored in `errno` and is a domain error.
`erange`	Stands for Error RANGE. Returns the value stored in `errno` if a range error occurs.
`errno`	Stands for ERRor Number. Defines a data object assigned a value larger than 0.

float.h

`dbl_dig`	Stands for DouBLe DIGit. Returns the number of decimal digits of precision for *double* type.
`dbl_epsilon`	Stands for DouBLe EPSILON. Returns the smallest value of x for *double* type.
`dbl_mant_dig`	Stands for DouBLe MANTissa DIGit. Returns the number of mantissa digits using base `flt_radix` for *double* type.
`dbl_max`	Stands for DouBLe MAX. Returns the largest finite representable *double* type value.
`dbl_max_10_exp`	Stands for DouBLe MAX 10 EXPonent. Returns the largest exponent integer x, where 10^x is a *double* type value.
`dbl_max_exp`	Stands for DouBLe MAX EXPonent. Returns the largest exponent integer x, where flt_radix^{x-1} is a *double* type value.
`dbl_min`	Stands for DouBLe MINimum. Returns the smallest value for a *double* type.

`dbl_min_10_exp`	Stands for DouBLe MINimum 10 EXPonent. Returns the smallest exponent integer x, where 10^x is a *double* type value.
`dbl_min_exp`	Stands for DouBLE MINimum EXPonent. Returns the smallest exponent integer x, where `flt_radix`$^{x-1}$ is a *double* type value.
`flt_dig`	Stands for FLoaT DIGit. Returns the number of decimal digits of precision for a `float` type value.
`flt_epsilon`	Stands for FLoaT EPSILON. Returns the smallest value x for a `float` type.
`flt_mant_dig`	Stands for FLoaT MANTissa DIGit. Returns the number of mantissa digits using base `flt_radix` for `float` type values.
`flt_max`	Stands for FLoaT MAXimum. Returns the largest finite value of a `float` type.
`flt_max_10_exp`	Stands for FLoaT MAXimum 10 EXPonent. Returns the largest exponent integer x, where 10^x is a `float` type value.
`flt_max_exp`	Stands for FLoaT MAXimum EXPonent. Returns the maximum integer x where `flt_radix`$^{x-1}$ is a `float` type value.
`flt_min`	Stands for FLoaT MINimum. Returns the smallest value of a `float` type.
`flt_min_10_exp`	Stands for FLoaT MINimum 10 EXPonent. Returns the smallest integer x where 10^x is a `float` type value.
`flt_min_exp`	Stands for FLoaT MINimum EXPonent. Returns the smallest exponent integer x, where `flt_radix`$^{x-1}$ is a `float` type value.
`flt_radix`	Stands for FLoaT RADIX. Returns the radix of all floating values.
`flt_rounds`	Stands for FLoaT ROUNDS. Describes the rounding mode in current use. A −1 means mode is not defined. A 0 means mode rounds towards 0. A 1 means mode rounds to nearest value. A 2 means mode rounds toward positive infinity. A 3 means mode rounds toward negative infinity.

213

`ldbl_dig`	Stands for Long DouBLe DIGit. Returns the number of decimal digits of precision for *long double* value.
`ldbl_epsilon`	Stands for Long DouBLe EPSILON. Returns the smallest value x for *long double* values.
`ldbl_mant_dig`	Stands for Long DouBLe MANTissa DIGit. Returns the number of mantissa digits using base `flt_radix` for *long double* types.
`ldbl_max`	Stands for Long DouBLe MAXimum. Returns the largest value for *long double* type.
`ldbl_max_10_exp`	Stands for Long DouBLe MAXimum 10 EXPonent. Returns the largest exponent integer x, where 10^x is a *long double* type value.
`ldbl_max_exp`	Stands for Long DouBLe MAXimum EXPonent. Returns the maximum integer x where `flt_radix`$^{x-1}$ is a *long double* type value.
`ldbl_min`	Stands for Long DouBLe MINimum. Returns the smallest value of a *long double* type.
`ldbl_min_10_exp`	Stands for Long DouBLe MINimum 10 EXPonent. Returns the smallest integer x where 10^x is a *long double* type value.
`ldbl_min_exp`	Stands for Long DouBLe MINimum EXPonent. Returns the smallest exponent integer x, where `flt_radix`$^{x-1}$ is a *long double* type value.

limits.h

`char_bit`	Stands for CHARacter BIT. Returns the largest value for the number of bits occupied by a data object of `char` type value.
`char_max`	Stands for CHARacter MAXimum. Returns the maximum value for a `char`. If `char` is negative, the value is the same as `shar_max`; otherwise, the value is same as `uchar_max`.
`char_min`	Stands for CHARacter MINimum. Returns the smallest value for `char`. If `char` is negative, the value is the same as `schar_min`; otherwise, it's 0.

`int_max`	Stands for INTeger MAXimum. Returns the largest value for `int` type values.
`int_min`	Stands for INTeger MINimum. Returns the smallest value for `int` type values.
`long_max`	Stands for LONG MAXimum. Returns the largest value for `long` type values.
`long_min`	Stands for LONG MINimum. Returns the smallest value for `long` type values.
`mb_len_max`	Stands for MultiByte LENgth MAXimum. Returns the largest number of characters that are contained in a multibyte character.
`schar_max`	Stands for Signed CHARacter MAXimum. Returns the largest value for *signed character* type values.
`schar_min`	Stands for Signed CHARacter MINimum. Returns the smallest value for *signed character* type values.
`shrt_max`	Stands for SHoRT MAXimum. Returns the largest value for *short* type values.
`shrt_min`	Stands for SHoRT MINimum. Returns the smallest value for *short* type values.
`uchar_max`	Stands for Unsigned CHARacter MAXimum. Returns the largest value for *unsigned character* type values.
`uint_max`	Stands for Unsigned INTeger MAXimum. Returns the maximum value for *unsigned integer* type values.
`ulong_max`	Stands for Unsigned LONG MAXimum. Returns the largest value for *unsigned long* type values.
`ushrt_max`	Stands for Unsigned SHoRT MAXimum. Returns the maximum value for *unsigned short* type values.

215

locale.h

`lc_all`	Returns the value in the *category* argument, which affects all categories.

lc_collate	Returns the value in the *category* argument, which affects the collation functions strcoll and strxfrm.
lc_ctype	Returns the value in the *category* argument, which affects the character handling and multibyte functions.
lc_monetary	Returns the value in the *category* argument, which affects the monetary values supplied by localeconv.
lc_numeric	Returns the value in the *category* argument, which affects the decimal point value returned by localeconv.
lc_time	Returns the value in the *category* argument, which affects the time conversion function supplied by strftime.
null	Returns a constant for the null pointer that serves as an address expression.

216

math.h

huge_val	Returns the value returned by another function on a range error. See information for the header file errnor.h.

setjmp.h

longmp	Forces a second return from the execution of a preceding setjmp function.
setjmp	Stuffs the current context value in the array jmp_buf defined by env and returns the value 0.

signal.h

sigabrt	Stands for SIGnal ABoRT. Returns the sig argument value for the abort signal.

sigpfe	Stands for SIGnal Function Procedure Error. Returns the `sig` argument value for the arithmetic error signal.
sigill	Stands for SIGnal ILLegal. Returns the `sig` argument value for an invalid execution signal.
sigint	Stands for SIGnal INTeractive. Returns the `sig` argument value for the asynchronous interactive attention signal.
sigsegv	Stands for SIGnal Store Value. Returns the `sig` argument value for the invalid storage access signal.
sigterm	Stands for SIGnal TERMination request. Returns the `sig` argument value for the asynchronous terminal request signal.
sig_dfl	Stands for SIGnal DeFauLt. Returns the `func` argument value to `signal` to declare the default signal handling value.
sig_err	Stands for SIGnal ERRor. Returns the `signal` return value declaring an erroneous call.
sig_ign	Stands for SIGnal IGNore. Returns the `func` argument value to `signal` to specify that the target environment is to ignore the signal.

217

starg.h

va_arg	Returns the value of the next argument in turn.
va_end	Lets a function return successfully by cleaning up the environment.
va_start	Stores information in the data object.

stddef.h

null	Returns a null pointer constant which is usable as an address.
offsetof	Stands for OFFSET OF bytes. Returns the offset value in bytes.

stdio.h

_IOFBF	Stands for Input Output Full BuFfer. Returns the value of the *mode* argument set to setvbuf to indicate full buffering.
_IOLBF	Stands for Input Output Line BuFfer. returns the value of the *mode* argument to setvbuf to indicated line buffering.
_IONBF	Stands for Input Output No BuFfer. Returns the value of the *mode* argument to setvbuf to indicate no buffering.
BUFSIZ	Stands for BUFfer SIZe. Returns the stream buffer used by setbuf.
EOF	Stands for End Of File. Returns the value used to signal the end of a file.
FILENAME_MAX	Stands for FILE NAME MAXimum size. Returns the maximum size array of character that you must provide to hold a file name string.
FOPEN_MAX	Stands for Files OPEN MAXimum number. Returns the maximum number of files that can be opened simultaneously in the environment.
L_tmpnam	Stands for List TMPNAM. Returns the number of characters required by the environment for representing temporary file names created by tmpnam.
NULL	Returns a null pointer constant usable as an address.
SEEK_CUR	Stands for SEEKing CURsor. Returns the value of the *mode* argument to indicate seeking of the file position indicator.
SEEK_END	Stands for SEEKing END of file. Returns that value of the *mode* argument to indicate seeking of the end of file marker.
stdin	Stands for STanDard INput stream. Returns a pointer to the data object that controls the standard input stream.
stdout	Stands for STanDard OUTput stream. Returns a pointer to the data object that controls the standard output stream.

stderr — Stands for STanDard ERRor. Returns pointer to the data object that controls standard error output stream.

TMP_MAX — Stands for TeMPorary file number MAXimum. Returns the maximum number of file names created by tmpnam.

stdlib.h

EXIT_FAILURE — Stands for EXIT FAILURE. Returns the value of status to exit that reports unsuccesful operation.

EXIT_SUCCESS — Stands for EXIT SUCCESS. Returns the value of status for exit that reports successful operation.

MB_CUR_MAX — Stands for MultiByte characters in CURrent locale MAXimum value. Returns the maximum number of characters contained in a multibyte character in the current locale.

NULL — Returns a null pointer usable as an address.

RAND_MAX — Stands for RAND MAXimum value. Returns the maximum value returned by rand.

219

Type Definitions

Every C expression has a type. The following type definitions are found in most ANSI C library header files.

setjmp.h

jmp_buf — Declares an array that holds information stuffed by the setjmp function and accessed by the longjmp function.

signal.h

sig_atomic_t   Stands for SIGnal ATOMIC operation. An assigning operator that alters a stored value.

stdarg.h

va_list   Stores information initialized by va_start and used by va_arg to access other arguments.

stddef.h

ptrdiff_t   Stores the result of subtracting two pointers.

size_t   Stores the result of the sizeof operator.

wchar_t   Stores a wide character.

220

stdio.h

FILE   Stores control information for a stream.

fpos_t   Holds the value of a file position indicator.

size_t   Holds the result of the sizeof operator.

stdlib.h

div_t   Holds the value returned by the function div.

C Programming Terminology

In This Appendix

The following list can serve as a short glossary of important words in programming (particularly C programming) that you can and should know if you want to become adept at C programming.

Terms

address   The number designating a particular section of computer memory.

algorithm   A collection of steps organized in such a way as to solve a problem.

ANSI   American National Standards Institute. A membership organization that develops voluntary technical national standards.

222

argument A value that can be passed between programs.

arithmetic operator Symbols designating arithmetic operations, such as + for addition and − for subtraction.

array An organized arrangement of data elements.

ASCII American Standard Code for Information Interchange, designating a commonly accepted code of characters.

backslash codes A series of codes used for formatting C programming output.

binary Designating two possible conditions, such as on and off. The binary notational system is composed of a string of 1s and 0s.

block A contiguous section of program code.

body The part of the program that contains instructions and statements.

Boolean Data that can be represented as yes/no or true/false.

buffer A section of computer memory reserved for data that's currently being processed.

char Character type data variable.

character An alphanumeric symbol, such as A or 1.

comments Textual description of a statement in a program. The text has no effect on the program.

compile To translate a high-level program, such as C, to a low-level language, such as machine code.

compiler A software device that compiles program code.

conditional statement A language statement that tests a condition.

constant A value that doesn't change.

CPU Central processing unit, or the microprocessor that performs most of the calculation in a computer.

curly braces Punctuation marks ({ and }) that signify limits to a block of program code.

data type	A type of data, such as character or numeric.
debugger	A software programs that helps locate and define bugs or mistakes in a software program.
decimal	A numeric notational system based on the number 10.
declaration	A statement that defines a type of data.
decrement	To count backwards or down in value, such as 5, 4, 3, 2, 1. See also *increment*.
DOS	Disk operating system, usually referring to microcomputer operating systems, such as PC DOS from IBM Corp. or MS-DOS from Microsoft Corp.
editor	Software program used to create, edit, and save text files, such as word processing files.
end-of-file marker	Code used to signify the end of a file. In PC DOS and MS-DOS, this code is ^Z.
EOF	Stands for *end-of-file marker*.
error checking	Checking for errors in a program, such as the syntax checker in a compiler. Also see *compiler*.
execute	Perform a single instruction or a series of instructions in a computer program.
floating point	The method for storing and calculating numbers where the decimal points don't line up but instead *float* to the degree of precision necessary.
function	A section of program code that performs a specific task.
global variable	A variable that's used by all sections of a program. See also *variables*.
header	The first part, or head, of a C program file that identifies the file and provides other information describing the file
hex system	See *hexadecimal system*.
hexadecimal system	A numeric notational system based on the number 16.

223

I/O	Input/output, or the transfer of data to and from the computer through devices, such as the keyboard and the terminal screen.
keyword	In C, a command term that serves as an instruction to the computer.
increment	To count upwards in value, such as 1, 2, 3, 4, 5. See also *decrement*.
input	See *I/O*.
integer	A whole number, such as 1, 3, 10, containing no decimal or fractional parts.
library	A collection of program and data files for use in programs that refer to the files.
linker	A software program that adapts a compiled program to a specific computer
local variable	A variable that's used by a specific section of a program. See also *variables*.
loop	A section of a computer program that repeats itself.
low-level language	A programming language that's close to machine code.
machine code	The native language of a computer's CPU.
modular programming	A method whereby sections of a computer program are indented and otherwise separated from each other so the programmer can make sense of the text commands.
output	See *I/O*.
pointer	In programming, a value that refers to another value in an array or other collection of data.
processor	See *CPU*.
pseudocode	A list of actions you want a program to perform written in vernacular language, not programming language.
RAM	Random access memory.
register	A circuit that holds values and addresses.

relational operator	Symbols designating comparisons between two values, such as = for *equal to* and >= for *greater than* or *equal to*.
sign	Designates a number as positive or negative.
statement	A descriptive phrase in a high-level programming language, such as C, that generates several machine code instructions when compiled.
string	A series of alphanumeric characters in a row.
terminator	A character that ends a string of characters.
text	Alphabetic and punctuation characters.
variable	A value that's prescribed by the programmer.

225

Index

229

231

233

235